How to Win the Meeting

How to Win the Meeting

Frank Snell

Hawthorn Books, Inc.
Publishers/New York
A HOWARD & WYNDHAM COMPANY

HOW TO WIN THE MEETING

Copyright© 1979 by Frank Snell. Copyright under International and Pan-American Copyright Conventions. All rights reserved, including the right to reproduce this book or portions thereof in any form, except for the inclusion of brief quotations in a review. All inquiries should be addressed to Hawthorn Books, Inc., 260 Madison Avenue, New York, New York 10016. This book was manufactured in the United States of America and published simultaneously in Canada by Prentice-Hall of Canada, Limited, 1870 Birchmount Road, Scarborough, Ontario.

Library of Congress Catalog Card Number: 78-61575

ISBN: 0-8015-3896-3

1 2 3 4 5 6 7 8 9 10

To Hilary, Nick, and Chris.
And particularly Majella,
who listens so well.

"Language best shows a man;
speak that I may see you."
—SAMUEL JOHNSON

Contents

Preface

"In my library are about a thousand volumes of biography . . . a rough calculation indicates that more of these deal with men who have talked themselves upward than with all the scientists, writers, saints, and doers combined. Talkers have always ruled. The smart thing is to join them."

—BRUCE BARTON

The meeting is the communications switchboard of every organization. It stands at the center of almost all company decisions. More than 75 percent of executive time is spent around the meeting room table. That's a lot of time out of a working life. But no one has found an alternative to the meeting and no one is likely to.

Thousands of books have been written on how to improve the meeting process, to make it work better. To come to decisions quicker, to come to more right decisions. But they haven't helped much. Why?

The reason is frighteningly simple. In spite of its wide and constant use, almost no one understands the meeting or the role of the meeting member.

Most books tell you that the meeting is a place for discussion, for people to trade ideas and merge thoughts, where philosophy and democracy go hand in hand. Wrong!

The meeting is a decision-making body, a place of force and persuasion. The meeting is where the best prepared member gets his ideas accepted because he is more direct, thinks more quickly, knows better how to use this communication forum. In school boards, political meetings, community action groups, each person must sell his point of view to bring about change and forward motion. In business, selling your point of view is called success. One sure path to that success is to WIN THE MEETING.

But are people who win the meeting just smarter, just naturally better speakers? Not necessarily. Think about it this way. The winning football team is the one that seems able, at will, to break away for that critical score. It's perfectly put together to do its job, to force its will upon its opponents. But is that really what a championship team is, a single force that overcomes its competitors? No. Like any organized group, it's a blending of a number of individual talents, kicking just a little bit better, blocking a little bit better, passing better, running the ball better. When all these talents are put together, that complex unit called the "team" wins.

The same is true of the person who wins the meeting. He wins not just because he's smarter than everyone else in the room. Frequently, he's not. It's not necessarily because he has more inside information or that he's favored by someone in authority. The person who wins the meeting is the person who takes advantage of a number of talents and techniques that when combined bring success in the meeting room.

As you read this book, some of the ways to win the conference will have you nodding because they're so obvious. Others will be completely new. The fact is that few have ever looked at the meeting this way before. It's new and very profitable ground.

And one thing is certain. Each idea in this book will definitely help you win the meeting.

How to Win the Meeting

Know the Agenda

Konrad Adenauer, the former chancellor of West Germany, was very specific about the ingredients of success.

"I insist on being smarter today than I was yesterday."

In order to win the meeting, this is about as good an objective as you can have. It is literally impossible to succeed in the meeting without constantly improving your knowledge. And an excellent place to start is with your next meeting, the one you've decided will not be like the rest, the one you've decided you will go to with a different philosophy—the one you've decided to win.

To walk into the meeting room without a careful, in-depth knowledge of what is to be discussed is like walking into the ring with Muhammad Ali. You're beaten before you begin.

To win the meeting you *must* have answers to the following questions:

Who called the meeting?
Why was the meeting called?
What is the background of the subject?
Where do you stand?
Can you win your point of view?
Are there vested interests?
Where do you hope to come out?

Let's start from the top.

Who Called the Meeting?

Obviously, all people in an organization are not at the same level. If the meeting was called by the president, it has a different meaning than if it was called by someone from PR. Try to determine whether it will be a controversial meeting or simply an informative one. Then ask yourself one more question. Was the meeting the idea of the person who called it, or is it being called for

4

someone else? Knowing the source of the meeting is critical if you are to determine its importance.

Why Was the Meeting Called?

Think about it for a moment. Is this a subject that has been rising to the surface for some time? Is it a hot potato? Is someone trying to force a decision? Why? Is it a pet peeve of the president? Know the "why" before you enter the room or you will get burned.

What Is the Background of the Subject?

Review the information you have in your head. Have there been previous meetings on the subject? What was the result? Who stood where on the subject and how strongly? Pull out background information from your files and read it over. Develop some support material. Just a few extra facts can win the meeting. Remember, you wouldn't be invited if they didn't expect you to contribute. And your contribution will be noticed. Don't get caught unprepared.

Where Do You Stand?

This is perhaps the single most important point to determine. Decades of meeting members have gone into the meeting with wishy-washy minds. Many go in with no position at all. Know *exactly* where you stand. Don't ever go to a meeting without a position clearly in your head. Without it you're totally vulnerable.

Can You Win Your Point of View?

This is an important question. Once you know where you stand on the subject under discussion, honestly determine whether it's possible for your point of view to prevail. There are many reasons why it might not. The president may have already voiced an opinion. A power group may be lined up in opposition to your position. The board of directors may have directed that certain steps be taken, steps you can't change. If you can't win, your strategy must be different. There's nothing practical about going down in flames unnecessarily. Perhaps you just play it more quietly, show a reasonable attitude. You might suggest that while the decision proceeds, additional information should be gathered (information that will later support your point of view). Perhaps you can suggest a test market to prove the validity of the idea before excessive money is spent. Perhaps a slight delay is warranted—until a more appropriate time. Just one warning. If you can't win, you must still be positive and friendly. Don't get pegged as being irascible and a bad loser. You'll have other meetings to go to—with the same people.

Are There Vested Interests?

Is the meeting beginning to reflect a known position of the president—or your boss—that is irreversible? Recognize that the jump to winning may be too high for you. It will do you very little good to put your head down and run against the wall like a bad-tempered child. To continue a struggle against impossible odds will just prove to everyone how bad your judgment is.

7

Where Do You Hope to Come Out?

This is one of the most important determinations that can improve your effectiveness in the meeting. It is certainly the most obvious bit of preparation one should make for the coming meeting. Unfortunately, it's also the one that's most often violated. No one, NO ONE should ever go into the meeting without clearly verbalizing what it is that he or she wants to accomplish.

Think of it this way. You go into a meeting in which you believe the decision to go national on a marketing plan is critical. You believe the plan has been well thought out and that delay will cause you to lose a big marketing opportunity. Go in deciding you will press constantly to win your point. You will pull out all the stops. You'll constantly return to your facts. You'll keep the meeting going when the discussion begins to wind down. You'll be well prepared with facts to support your case. You'll never falter or show any signs of compromise. You'll make it clear you want to get a "go" decision . . . Now!

8

Let's take another case. You decide the boss is against a suggestion to revise the profit-sharing plan—an idea you support. You've thought it all out and you decide it's literally impossible for you to win out over him (and the many people who will support his point of view). You just don't have the ammunition . . . right now! So, you know where you want to come out. You decide to follow the military wisdom of withdrawing and fighting another day on better ground, with better weapons.

Now, no one in the meeting knows of your plan. To them, you are there to win. Strangely enough, most meeting members think that all present have the same simplistic view of pressing for their viewpoint to prevail. But your plan is different. It is a plan you made *before* you came into the meeting.

You plan to let the meeting progress, to inject thoughts, to comment on problems, to suggest ideas—smoothly, easily, unemotionally. But toward the end of the meeting you'll begin to suggest the need for information that you think should be reviewed or for advice from some consultant who should be heard. The boss agrees because he's against the revised plan anyway. Soon you have his support.

9

Slowly, you ease the meeting to a close by withdrawing the motive power, by pointing to the fact that the question will be easy to resolve in the *next* meeting. You have prevented the subject from being sealed and the group from becoming committed, with no future opportunity to get it reversed.

There are dozens of positions you might wish to take. The preceding one was a simple delay of the meeting. You might want to get other people involved in the discussion because you believe it will help your case. You might want another meeting because your chief opponent will be on vacation. You may want to hold off until a new measurement of sales comes in, a measurement that will help your cause.

In short, perhaps the most common failure of meeting members is that they go in unprepared; not only unprepared on facts, but unprepared as to what the meeting is about, where they stand on the subject under discussion, and how to effect a desired solution.

Review this list before you go to your next meeting:

Who called the meeting?
Why was the meeting called?

What is the background of the subject?
Where do you stand?
Can you win your point of view?
Are there vested interests?
Where do you hope to come out?

Use the advice Benjamin Franklin gave Joseph Priestly, who wrote him asking him for a point of view on a particular subject. Franklin said,

> "I cannot tell you *what* to determine, but if it please you, I will tell you *how*."

Take advantage of this simple checklist. It will help you win the meeting.

11

Where You Sit Can Help You Win

When you go to a football game, you want a seat on the fifty-yard line so you can see all the action. At the concert, you ask for a center seat in the front of the orchestra to get a true balance of the music. And think how careful you are about the table you're given on that evening you go out to dinner—nothing but the best will do, near the window or near the dance floor. You want the best seats because they'll let you see better, hear better, make you feel more comfortable, more important. And all for a nonpressured, social situation.

What about a far more important situation? Your business situation? Your committee groups? Your town leadership councils? What are you doing about your seating position in the meeting?

How to Win the Meeting

For some reason, the two places in which many people try to be invisible are the classroom and the meeting room. In the classroom they sit as far back as possible (probably to stay out of the professor's field of vision). In the meeting they frequently take the seat that can effectively put them into the land of the forgotten.

Why? Two reasons probably. One, most people who go to meetings don't understand how important the meeting really is to their personal careers. At best they consider it just another function of their everyday work. Besides, they feel more comfortable in the shadows. These are two bad mistakes.

For someone who wants to improve his image, increase his effectiveness, strengthen his future, there is a huge opportunity in just where you sit in the meeting room itself.

Don't be invisible!

Plan where you *want* to sit before you go into the meeting. Where you sit can have a great effect on whether or not your ideas get attention, on whether or not your thoughts prevail, on whether or not you win the meeting.

Here are some simple rules of thumb to help you avoid the onus of invisibility.

If the meeting table is long and narrow, try to sit at the end opposite the boss or on the side close to the leader.

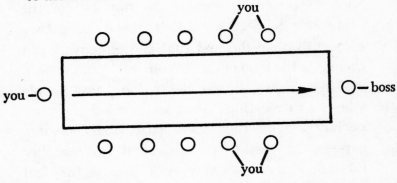

Never get caught (unless you're late and you shouldn't be!) in the following no-man's-land where your visual contact with the boss or leader is materially obstructed.

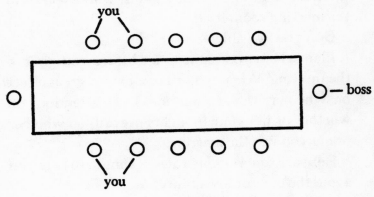

How to Win the Meeting

If the table is rectangular with wings and the boss sits in the middle of the long side, you sit at either end so that you'll be talking across the bare table, not through someone's head.

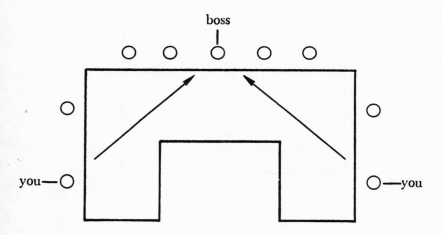

If the meeting table is square or rectangular, the best place to sit is opposite the boss (or the most important person) in the meeting. In the meeting, it's difficult enough to fight for verbal attention when you want to make a statement. You certainly don't want to have to struggle for visibility.

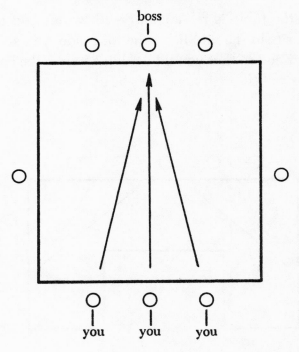

Let me add one qualification to what I've just said about seating. Watch and study the decision maker, the leader. If he happens to be the kind who depends on the people who sit beside him, if he whispers to them and asks for their points of view, get yourself seated next to him in a meeting. This is the "advisor" position and it can be very effective.

16

How to Win the Meeting

Watch for this tendency in your leaders and take advantage of it. It can work well for you.

Whatever you do, don't sit with your superior between you and the boss. In this position the results are almost always bad. The boss may ask a question and direct it your way. But your superior is in a position to field it and leave you invisible. If you were seated across the way, you could add to your superior's statement and the whole table would move their eyes and attention to you. Remember, what you're trying to do is to be highly visible because with visibility comes attention and with attention comes authority and recognition.

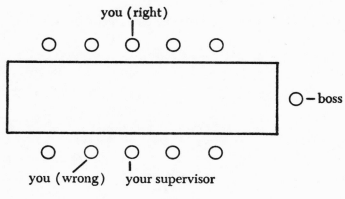

Don't sacrifice a good position at the meeting table by coming late. The grand entrance may be an effective way to come to the ball, but at the business meeting it will simply get you a seat behind the water cooler.

If there is visual aid equipment, be sure you don't take a position behind it. You don't want to take second place to a movie projector.

Remember, the place you sit in the meeting is a large factor in determining your image and effectiveness. You must be very visible and very available to exploit the discussion, to answer the questions and move the meeting. If you follow these suggestions, you'll have a better chance of having your ideas listened to and of winning the meeting.

P.S.: Whatever you do, don't sit in the boss's seat!

Listen Harder Than Anyone Else

Listen to this conversation that goes on between Alice and Humpty Dumpty in *Through the Looking Glass.*

> " '. . . How old did you say you were?'
> "Alice made a short calculation, and said,
> 'Seven years and six months.'
> " 'Wrong!' Humpty Dumpty exclaimed triumphantly.
> 'You never said a word like it!'
> " 'I thought you meant, "How old *are* you?" '
> Alice explained.
> " 'If I'd meant that, I'd have said it,' said
> Humpty Dumpty."

As much as I like Alice, Humpty Dumpty was right. What's more important, Lewis Carroll is making a point that all of us who want to succeed in speaking should pay careful attention to. In fact, we can make a pretty safe statement here: The individual who learns to listen harder in a speaking situation—especially in the meeting—has a far better chance of seeing his point of view prevail.

I urge you to listen harder than anyone else. You will have a better chance of winning the meeting.

Speaking well in a meeting has always been thought of as the primary goal. It has been assumed that the person who masters this will succeed. Not necessarily true. It's *equally* as important to listen well—perhaps even more so, since practically no one does it.

Anyone who has ever listened to a pro tennis player in an after-match interview will invariably hear talk of how important it is to maintain "concentration" during the match. Without concentration it's literally impossible to win a top competition. What is true of tennis is even truer of the meeting. Tennis is an activity of physical motion, but the meeting is made up of ephemeral words put forth on nothing more substantial than air. If in tennis you must keep your eye on the ball, in speaking and listening, you must keep your ear on the "idea." Here are some things you can do to listen better.

Always keep your ear on the mainstream of the meeting. There may be tributaries from this idea, but track carefully the central flow. It will then be easier for you to see tangents, those thoughts that dart off from the central idea. Listen carefully when this happens and watch to see if the meeting is diverted by them. Eventually, like tributaries, they dry up.

Pay attention everlastingly. Nothing can reduce your chances of winning the meeting more than getting off into a splinter discussion. If some meeting "whisperer" tries to draw you off into conversation, suggest (pleasantly) that there's a vital point that's just come up and you're particularly interested in it. Show you're listening hard! Naturally, there is one exception: If the boss wants to whisper something in your ear, you really can't turn that off. Listen. You gain authority by the boss's attention.

21

How to Win the Meeting

Don't ever leave an important meeting. Unless you don't care about the end results. It's like leaving a chess match and allowing your opponent to make as many moves in the interim as he wants. When you return, the game will be over. Many business executives make the unfortunate mistake of having their secretaries bring a message to the meeting telling them that there's a phone call or that their lunch date is waiting. Don't do it. When you leave the meeting room, chances are your position will leave with you. It's not only bad manners, it's a good way to lose the meeting.

Spot selective listeners. Every group has meeting members who hear just what they want to hear—one-way listeners. Watch for them. When you watch a football game, you see the quarterback searching out the opponent's formation as he calls the plays. Frequently a shift in the opposing team will call for a completely different play. You should do the same. Watch for the people who only hear what they want to. They're usually easy to cope with because their minds are so inflexible. Decide whether to move around their center of resistance or to play to the narrowness of their view, and then move in for the score. Don't tangle with them. Others will have noticed their rigidness too. Emotional conflict with this type only weakens your own image.

Listen carefully for the misunderstanding of a word. Ego makes us believe that what we say is absolutely clear. Naturally. We all grew up with the same language; why shouldn't we all understand each other easily. Right? Wrong!

Language is tricky. One communications teacher said it was easier to pass a peanut then to pass an idea. To put it simply, words do not mean the same thing to all people—like these two women discussing the building of a new running track for the high school field:

> Woman #1: "I suppose the *diplomatic* thing would be to invite the school principal to the meeting—"
> Woman #2: "I have no desire to be diplomatic or 'slippery,' as I suppose you mean—"
> Woman #1: "I didn't mean that at all," etc.

Or two teachers discussing the upcoming senior dance:

23

TEACHER #1: "Or we could do what Steve suggests. It's more *radical*, but—"
TEACHER #2: "There you go again. Steve, the harebrained one, the radical . . ."

Watch out for the misunderstood words. They can keep you circling the same subject for hours—and arguing most of the time.

Pick out the role players. Every meeting group is a microcosm of the world about us. Each contains the logical one, the follower, the one who pretends to be the hero, the one who rebels against the system. Pick them out and watch them as the meeting progresses. The Good Guy usually argues for the good "of all concerned" and follows the path of good will for everyone. The Rebel wants to break new ground. Sweep away all that's associated with the past. He's frequently tied to the impractical because he wants change more than someone who's practical. The Follower does just that. Sways with the verbal wind of the meeting.

Listen and pick out these prototypes. Like the quarterback mentioned earlier, when you know how your opponents will act, you can direct your efforts to winning your points.

The meeting is a complex interchange of words and ideas. A jostling for position, confrontation, acceptance, success, failure. Use the foregoing suggestions to gain an advantage over the other meeting members. Understanding the subtleties of the meeting room arena gives you an important power advantage.

See Yourself As
Others See You

"Oh wad some pow'r the giftie gie us
To see oursels as others see us!"
—ROBERT BURNS

Body language is a popular subject. Many books
have been written about how people react
physically in various situations. Body language
has something to tell us about the meeting, about
how it can help or hurt you win your point of
view.

First of all, your appearance certainly has an
effect on people. Look at airline pilots—tall and
handsome. It doesn't make them better pilots, but
it does give travelers a lot of reassurance. It should
come as no surprise that big, tall, handsome
people are expected to speak with authority and

force. Small, frail people must realize that they have to overcome the initial impression that what they say will be indecisive, tentative. It may not be true, but this is a fact of life.

Happily, it's in the hands of the individual to change those poor impressions. Many small people quickly establish themselves as authorities, forces to be recognized. Napoleon is the obvious example. It can be done if you recognize the importance of body action and understand what it can do for you.

Let's turn to the meeting and see what body actions you should use . . . and avoid.

How to Sit

You can't expect to win the meeting with weak thoughts, a weak voice, weak ideas, or weak words. Don't expect to win it with a flabby appearance, either. A lot of meeting members seem to believe that a loose, sprawling appearance says that they're friendly and cooperative, willing to work with the other members. Wrong. A loose, sprawling appearance says that you have a loose, sprawling mind and that what you will say isn't worth listening to. Sit up straight. Don't be rigid, of course, but let your body show that your mind is alert and tuned in, not oozy.

How to Use Your Eyes

You've all seen how directors establish the character of villains in the movies, how their eyes move when asked a direct question. Their eyes shift, they look at you sideways. Fact is, we've been judging people by their eyes since man first walked upright. It's said that jade dealers in the East know how much to ask for a piece of jade by watching the eyes of the person they're trying to sell to. Depending on how the eyes respond, the price is set.

Your eyes count in the meeting too. Look at the people around the table. Look at each one. Speak a line or two to each one. Be direct. Don't flit. Shiftiness says uncertainty, deviousness. Look directly ahead, not out of the side of your eyes. The direct look will give what you have to say "body strength."

Another thing about eyes. They're very revealing of inner desires. Many speakers look in an almost appealing way to other members of the meeting. They have a hound dog look as if begging for approval. Don't do it. Say what you have to say objectively and openly. Don't ever plead for acceptance with your eyes. It will weaken what you have to say and your opponents will take advantage of this perceived weakness.

How to Use Your Arms

Normally. That's how to use them. Don't try to hide them as though they are obscene. Don't sit with them folded rigidly across your chest. It will say just that—rigidity. Let your arms rest easily, naturally, on the table before you. Assume your position as though you belonged there. You do!

How to Use Your Hands

This is very important. Hands go with words, no matter what you were told when you were growing up. Use your hands in the meeting. Point. Gesture. Use your hands to explain shape, size, direction, intensity (the higher the hands are raised, the greater the intensity). Hands are part of you and will make what you have to say more compelling and believable. Be certain, however, to avoid fiddling. Don't play with anything on the table before you—such as a pencil or a paper clip. And don't doodle. If you do, the others will find themselves concentrating on what you're doing and not a bit on what you are saying.

Think about body language. Don't go to your next meeting without considering the best use of your whole body. The way you look will help you win the meeting.

As the essayist Ralph Waldo Emerson said,

"What you are thunders so loud I can't hear what you say."

Always
Leave Them Laughing

Here's a simple idea that is rarely thought of by speakers in a meeting. It's simple in thought, but surprisingly complex in nature. It's the idea of winning the meeting by taking a light swipe at yourself—just enough to allow your humanity to show through.

It should be obvious that the meeting is a place where you find nature in the raw. There, points of view are hammered home ruthlessly, ideas are fought for viciously, advantages are won and exploited, losers are pushed aside. The meeting in today's world is all seriousness. People go in to win and will do anything to achieve that win There's little given away easily. It's no laughing matter. Or is it?

The president of one of the world's largest advertising agencies taught me a lesson that I've always remembered. He taught me you can win your point *and* the meeting with the simplest technique. Make a joke about yourself.

I remember him in a meeting telling how he was sure that his entire career was made by bosses who put him in jobs he knew nothing about to keep him from changing anything. And that now they were trying him out as president . . . another job they thought he knew nothing about.

The response from his colleagues was astonishing. The temperature of a rather tense meeting cooled. People laughed out loud. Points of view were conceded. Everything ran smoothly. And the president's point was, of course, carried.

Later, I asked him how he came to use this technique. He said that he always found it worked well to show others that you were human, that you didn't have to protect yourself, that maybe everyone was taking himself too seriously. After that I watched him carefully and found him winning his points even in the tightest of situations (appearing before congressional committees, for instance). And he used this technique over and over in presentations.

The result was invariably the same. His listeners liked him—and did what he asked. Telling a light, warm joke about yourself is an excellent weapon to help win the meeting.

Get on the Positive Bandwagon

The "force of the positive" is one of the most powerful and least thought about weapons you can bring to the meeting. Looking on the bright side may seem unimportant, but in meetings, as in life, there is an overriding yearning for a positive outlook. If you doubt it, look at the success and number of books on the positive approach to life and philosophy.

The positive force isn't at all mystical. It doesn't call for extensive new knowledge. It requires no unusual talent beyond common sense. From a strategic point of view, the positive outlook is simple to apply. From a practical point of view it's a great way to see your ideas accepted and put into action.

We live in a complicated world that gets more complicated every day. It's becoming more crowded, more expensive, alternatives are shrinking, people are becoming testier, more negative. It's heavily downbeat. And all this is reflected in our communications with one another, whether in discussion with your daughter's school advisor, or in a meeting with the executive committee of your company. This negativeness, like everything in life, can be turned around to have a positive side. If you stress the positive it will make you stand out, give you an advantage.

You've probably been to this kind of meeting:

BILL: "Looks like we've got a *nasty* problem here."

JOHN: Yes, and it's been *difficult* for some time."

MELISSA: "I just heard that the packaging for the product is *delayed* now too. . . ."

NEGATIVE . . . NEGATIVE . . . NEGATIVE

Imagine the response to someone who said:

"Last night I thought about this subject and I have a little game plan. I really believe we can solve this problem quite easily. My plan shows that if we move positively, we'd have control of the market for almost a year. That's a lot of sales!

35

And the money we take in will allow us to correct other simple problems. Who can tell? This may be a year for good bonuses."

Positive. You offer to help to solve the problem. You tell everyone to cheer up. Don't be negative. And, you say it nicely. Finally, you use the greatest motivation of all. "The Big I." The promise of reward for each person in the room.

The difference between the negative approach and the positive approach is little short of dramatic. Listen to this leader who starts the meeting out with the positive force:

"I was informed that the problem we're going to discuss is tough and that it's been plaguing people in this company for years. I told them that it can't be too tough for this group. We'll just turn up our brain power and solve it. It's that simple. Oh, by the way, I have a meeting with the executive VP in an hour. So let's get at it."

Positive thinking. Positive speaking. Use this technique to make yourself someone people turn to when they want something done. You can't solve all the physical problems, but you can solve the mental ones. Avoid the downbeat approach. Who needs it? Life is difficult enough.

The positive will have a powerful effect on your listeners. They will reward you for it. Do the following in your next meeting:

1. Watch for negative statements and move in to get the meeting on the positive track.

2. Listen for downbeat statements that block solution thinking. Unblock them.

3. Downplay difficult parts of the meeting. Solve simple problems first; it can set a pattern.

4. Offer solutions and hope when others offer difficulty and despair.

5. Hold out carrots—rewards for all if a solution is found.

6. Offer to take on problems yourself. It will lighten the tone of the meeting.

7. On a truly difficult problem be realistic, but never gloomy.

8. Refuse to be negative. Exploit the force of the positive!

The 1–2–3 System
for Presenting Ideas

Plutarch, in first-century Greece, said that Phocion, the Greek, compared the speeches of Leosthenes to cypress trees.

"They are tall and comely, but bear no fruit."

Unfortunately, this is not a problem that died with the ancient Greeks. Putting an idea into words with meaning and impact is without doubt the most difficult thing the human creature is asked to do. In the face of it people with knowledge and experience become tongue-tied. People with conviction stumble. People with dedication flounder. *How* people frame their ideas too often says to the listeners that they really don't know what they're talking about. Unfortunately, information is useless unless it can be passed on. And information that needs to be passed verbally is doubly difficult. Add to this the fact that in a meeting situation your ideas are restricted by time and other psychological pressures and your thoughts are in competition with those of other people in the room—all of whom want to win the meeting.

You can never expect to win unless your spoken ideas have impact, substance, and conviction. Happily, there's a way this can be done if you apply the following formula for effective speaking. I call it the 1-2-3 System for presenting your ideas. Use it, it can give you a giant advantage.

Most meeting members have no real idea of the sequence of thoughts in a meeting. They just never think about it. They simply respond to something that's been said. They agree, or add something new, or just swim languidly through the warm flow of words. It's not that they don't have something to say. They think they're doing that. It's just that they have never spent time working out how to put a verbal contribution together. If you do, you'll come to the meeting with a big advantage over all the others. It will give you another opportunity to help win the meeting. Here's how to do it.

All ideas put forth in the meeting, like ideas in every form of communication should have three parts:

    1. a statement of a premise; of where you stand on a subject;

    2. a couple of pieces of information to prove what you have said;

    3. a *re*statement of where you stand, to make certain that your listeners didn't become so interested in the "proof" that they forgot the premise.

It's as simple as that. And it goes like this:

STATEMENT . . . PROOF . . . RESTATEMENT

STATEMENT

"I definitely believe the product is going to succeed."

PROOF

"Our first two Nielsen shares were above objective. That means the consumer is taking the product off the shelves."

40

Proof

"Sales are increasing substantially. Latest numbers here show a 45 percent increase over the preceding week."

Proof

"Reports from the sales force are enthusiastic."

Restatement

"Therefore, I firmly believe the product is going to be a success."

Simple? Yes. But how few people do it. Here's another example.

Statement

"The curriculum of the high school should *not* add technical courses at the expense of courses in the humanities."

Proof

"The world these kids are moving into is complicated. Their biggest choices will not be whether they can repair a car. It will be whether they can repair a world."

Proof

"It's shocking that in the last year fewer mind-expanding humanities courses were taught in the high schools of this country than there were forty years ago. Do we believe the world has become simpler?"

PROOF

"Ethics are weaker at home. Fewer and fewer people are influenced by the church. Are we to remove humanities and ethics from the school as well?"

RESTATEMENT

"Therefore, I say we must not reduce the teaching of humanities in this school."

If you take advantage of this technique, if you present your responses in meetings in the 1–2–3 System way, your chances of winning are far, far greater. Your ideas will be listened to. They will be understood. They will be remembered. And you will become a mover.

Success in the meeting is never by chance. It is as easy as 1–2–3.

What's in It for Me?

There are two specific motivations you will perceive in action in every meeting; two drives that have a determining effect on how the individual meeting member will act, how he will vote, and how desperately he will hold to a particular point of view. If you don't recognize these two motivations, you are missing critical information that can guide your actions in the meeting, information that you can use to your very great advantage. I call it "the two-way pull."

This is how it works. All the people sitting blankly across from you at the meeting table have two objectives in mind. One is to solve the problem before them, to dig out the facts, to sort them, and to piece them back together in a forceful conclusion—A conclusion that will be of value to the company they work for, the club they belong to, the community board they serve, the political party they support. This is a major drive: to find a solution for the problem they are wrestling with and make their group or business more successful.

But this is just one motivation, the lesser of two. There is another big drive that overshadows the one just described. And the core of the drive we're talking about is called *me*. It asks what will my action do to *me*? What will what I have to say do to *my* position? What will people think about *me* if I say that? What will the boss think? *My* colleagues? *My* friends? What will it mean to *my* future?

When people talk together, they don't seek only to solve group problems. The world we live in simply isn't like that. The protection of ME, the ambition of ME, the future of ME all come *before* the responsibility to company, club, board, group. A long way before.

So, then, each individual has two objectives; one to do his job well, and the other to protect himself and position himself favorably in the world he lives in. And if he must make a choice between the two, the choice will certainly be with the *me* drive.

But how can this help you win the meeting? How can this insight be applied when you sit down with others to talk?

Recognize these two drives and never forget the immense pull of "me." Accept the fact that this attitude exists and plays a giant part in the actions of people.

Understand that the "me" drive has you in tow, too. Analyze your own emotional behavior when you're talking with others: why you may avoid bringing a subject to a head; why personal drives get between you and the company good; why you feel threatened and are tempted to strike back. This striking back can cost you dearly—in your job, with your colleagues, with your friends—and gain little. One good technique is to recognize when you are moving into the "me" area. When you feel your judgment, authority, position, etc., is being challenged. Sit back a moment. Take a deep breath before you respond. You can pursue the "me" drive, but do it logically, without emotion.

Learn to recognize the "me" response in others.

45

There are a number of things to look for. For instance, "me" responses frequently occur from a person under attack. You can see the blood run to his head, his eyes sharpen, his face becoming drawn. He has been threatened and his response may very well lose him credibility. Also, look for the "cave" syndrome; when the meeting member pulls back into the mouth of the cave and prepares to ward off attackers, prepares to defend his territory against marauders.

One highly visible happening that says "here comes a 'me' " is when someone you know well takes a position 180 degrees from where you know he has always stood. He may be protecting his job or the favor with which his boss holds him, or his hopes for growth in the company. Don't be surprised when this type of response comes through. This person has just decided it's time to succumb to the "me" drive. At this moment, company, friends, and colleagues are all secondary.

How can this knowledge add to your effectiveness in the meeting? A number of ways.

Recognizing a "me" response will help you

understand many statements you'll hear in meetings. If you know where they come from, you can handle them better. Just knowing the world is not all "reason" is to know a great deal.

It's of little value to confront directly someone evidencing the "me" drive. It will only push him deeper into it. You could force him to make a fool of himself under pressure, but this is risky business. Like a carousel, business keeps coming around again. Better to try to move around a person like this; let him have his position. You may create a friend for the many times you meet in the future.

I believe in the "soft" defense with most "me" situations. Take a tack that neutralizes the response. Move around the statement to another approach. You'll often find you'll get support for trying to move the meeting forward logically.

Don't be too quick to jump at a "me" response. Think about it a moment. You may be refuting the president of the company.

Most important of all, know when the "me" response is coming out of your own mouth. Know when you're saying what you intend to be saying

47

. . . and why. It will give you more control, make you approach the meeting more logically. If you must make a "me" response (and everyone does), know that you are—and why.

The Greek philosopher Epictetus said it well:

> "What disturbs and alarms man are not the things, but his opinions and fancies about the things."

Make Your Numbers Live

When you write a letter, you are urged to get the number of the street, the number of the house, and certainly the zip code correct. And don't forget your return address.

Numbers.

When you rent a car, nine-tenths of the form you complete is in numbers. Your address, your license number, your credit card number, the dollar rate for the day, the cost per mile, gas charges per mile, cost of insurance, license plate number of the car, the space the car is parked in ... all in numbers.

We live in a world of numbers. We are utterly dependent upon them. We are drowning in them. In the face of this, isn't it strange that when we present an idea to a group of listeners, we do it head down and rushing forward, flooding our listeners with numbers . . . numbers . . . numbers. Ah, but you say, in spite of the fact that there are too many numbers, they still remain an indispensable way to talk about things. True. You must use numbers to communicate in today's world. But you must also learn *how* to use them.

Think about it this way. Numbers are symbols. Like the red light that says stop, or the clenched fist that says communist, or the stars and stripes that say America—so too numbers. Numbers stand for things; are symbols for facts. Like the distance from the ground to the top of the Empire State Building or the amount of money in the Morgan bank vault or the number of people in India.

When you use numbers in the meeting, there are two problems. There are often too many numbers, and the fact that they *remain* numbers often means they are not easily grasped by the listeners. In both instances the numbers become useless and your effort is seriously weakened.

Here are some suggestions that will make your use of numbers stand out from the pack. Be more visible, be livelier, stay in the minds of your listeners longer and make them more inclined to follow what you say in the meeting.

Use numbers with discretion, never when they're not needed. And use as few as will do the job. Spewing out numbers will only make your listeners close their mental shutters and let your thoughts slide painlessly by. Choose a few critical, sharp numbers and hammer them home to prove your point.

Make your numbers live. Take them out of their abstract, dull form and make them talk to your listeners. For instance, you could say:

> "Our cost of hiring temporary secretaries for last year was $600,090. That's a lot of money."

That's fact but hardly commanding. Why not say it in a way that will involve your listeners. Say it in "people" language. Bring your numbers down to the listeners.

> "Our cost of hiring temporary secretaries for last year was $600,090. Looked at another way, if that money were added to profit, *it would add 15 cents a share to our dividends.*"

That's more vital; easier to listen to; easier to grasp; easier to accept. Personal.

51

Focus on a single number. If you have more than ·one number, use your vocal finger to point out the one that's most important to your thought.

"Factory sales are up 22 percent. Warehouse withdrawals up 13 percent. The category is up 17 percent. Unfortunately, the Nielsen for our brand is off 2.5 percent. *And that's what I'd like you to remember—that 2.5 percent.* Because that means the consumer is not taking enough of our product off the shelf."

Translate your numbers. Your listeners will respond best to numbers in the meeting when they are led along by your thinking. So help them.

"If we're to be in the household cleansing product area, we must have a liquid laundry detergent. It's a tough market and competition is stiff, but look at the rewards. *One share point of volume is worth twenty million dollars.*"

Dramatize your numbers. Listeners understand numbers best when they're translated into everyday existence, when the idea is placed side by side with something they know well, something they can visualize.

"Living in the world of the 1970s, we have the idea that today we make everything bigger and better. I'm not sure either of these is true. Certainly not the bigger part. For instance, *in the 1920s we built a lighter-than-air airship that carried more than two hundred people and was as long as three football fields.*"

Here's a fun dramatization of numbers before the first Ali/Spinks heavyweight fight. James Tuite, sportswriter, said Spinks was fighting for $320,000, or 355,556 bologna sandwiches.

And one final example of the effectiveness of dramatizing your numbers to make them live:

"The administration is asking all the industry in the state of New York to convert from oil to coal. That's not a good idea. If only 4 percent were to use sulphur coal, *we would put ten pounds of sulphur in the air for every man, woman, and child in the state.*"

In summary, everyone responds to an idea that strikes a spark. Strike some sparks when you present numbers in your next meeting. Your chances of being remembered—and followed—will be increased tenfold.

Call in Some "Big Guys" to Fight by Your Side

There is no reason in the world to feel that you're alone and isolated in the meeting room. No, I don't just mean isolated from those adversaries lined up so formally. They're always there. I mean you have presences sitting close by your side waiting for you to call on them to help you prove your point, to help you win the meeting. Unfortunately, they're seldom thought of, and therefore rarely given the chance to support your position.

Just who are these people? You know them all: Shakespeare, Voltaire, Churchill, Roosevelt, Tolstoy, Caesar, Alexander Pope, Ben Franklin, W. C. Fields, Jack Benny, and thousands more! They're an impressive group. With *big* influence.

They're all there leaning forward anxiously, waiting for you to call on them to speak in your behalf.

Just about every idea—on just about every subject—has been expressed at some time in the past. At various times throughout history, famous people have talked about everything and in amazingly concise ways. This gives you a library full of support—both verbal and logical—that you should be using. If you're not, you're limiting your opportunities to win the meeting.

For example. Let's assume you're in an advertising discussion and one of your opponents takes the position that advertising is wasteful. You could call the department store tycoon and financial wizard John Wanamaker to your side and quote him as follows:

> "Sure, that's true. But, as John Wanamaker said, 'I *know* that half of the advertising I do is wasted. The trouble is, I don't know *which* half.' "

Touché.

Or if someone on the school board complains that a new course being proposed is too difficult; that the students might fail it, ask Lord Bacon to speak for you:

55

"Perhaps, but as Lord Bacon pointed out, 'though success be indeed more pleasing, yet failure, frequently is no less informing.' "

It may be that you're in a local political board meeting and the question of directives from the party in Washington comes up. You want to take a strong stand against it. Call on Thomas Jefferson to step forward and speak for your point of view:

"I happen to agree with Jefferson, who said, 'Were we directed from Washington when to sow and when to reap, we would soon want for bread.' "

There's tremendous power in the pithy, sharp statements of famous people. If you don't take advantage of them, you're missing a great opportunity.

One of the reasons that quotes from famous people work so well is that they operate in a realm divorced from strict fact or reason. They operate with all the emotional punch that combines an idea well stated by a person well known and highly respected. Get yourself a book and jot down every good, clear, incisive quote you come upon. Add a book of familiar quotations to your library. When you need a big piece of support, you can reach into your mental barrel and pull out just the right weapon.

George Washington, Samuel Johnson, Mark Twain, Woody Allen, W. H. Auden, Abraham Lincoln, William Buckley, Red Smith . . . please stand up and identify yourselves to your audience!

Impact by Analogy

I'm always amazed at how easily some meeting participants can win over all the others by using a simple technique you'd think everyone knew. But strangely, the idea of using this technique rarely occurs to most people. So learn this persuader and use it. You'll have a big advantage over your colleagues.

What I'm suggesting is simply that you compare what you're talking about with something else; something that makes what you have to say clearer; makes your idea simple and sharp; makes it stick in the listener's mind when other ideas have faded away.

Whenever I hear a good analogy, comparison,

or simile used, I'm astounded at the effect it has. You can look around the meeting table and actually see people nodding their heads in agreement. Because what you said is so *clear*; because it has focused your idea in their minds so vividly.

Suppose the meeting has been circling around a subject endlessly and you want to point this out to the group. You could say:

"I suggest we may have exhausted this subject."

Which would be average dull for meetings.

Or you could say:

"This subject is dry. If we continue, I suggest *we're only making a big shoe for a small foot.*"

You *know* which of these two statements the group will remember. Why? Because the human mind *likes* words. Man is a verbal creature and likes to hear words used well and originally. It pleases the listener to hear an imaginative comparison. It will go a long way toward making your listener agree with you. And that's what the meeting is all about.

Imagine a meeting in which a great many

suggestions have been offered and still more are coming. You think there have been too many and you want to stop them. You could say:

> "I don't think the answer depends on the sheer number of solutions."

Or you could put forth a good, strong comparison that makes the logic of your statement so clear that it's irresistible. You could say:

> "Good solutions don't come just from the number of suggestions. *The restaurant with the longest menu doesn't necessarily have the best food.*"

All around the table people will be mentally nodding because of the brevity and originality of your thought. There's big power in a simple statement. Many of these simple statements have been with us for hundreds or thousands of years and we're still quoting them.

One more example. Let's suppose someone in the group is suggesting that another, boring, detailed study be done before you move to build the new school gymnasium. You think you're already wallowing in studies. In fact, you're determined not to stand for the delay. You can

60

hammer your point home with a telling comparison like this:

"I'm sure another study would make some of us feel warm all over. But to me *another study would be like a cyprus tree. Big and handsome, but with no fruit.* I say let's get directly to the plan that will bear fruit. We should build the gym now!"

Get yourself a book and jot down every good analogy you hear or read. They're invaluable. You'll use them time and again. Coupled with the other suggestions in this book, they're another powerful lever to topple the meeting your way.

The American Way
of Saving Face

The meeting members are sparring cautiously across the table like fighters, feeling one another out, not committing to a definite point of view just yet. Everyone wants to find out where the others stand—and most importantly, where the VIP stands. Bill makes a statement about the sales volume in the Cleveland district. As soon as he makes it, you know he's wrong. Now's the time for you to go for the jugular. Go in for the kill. Right?

Wrong! Most companies are made up of teams that talk together in meetings all the time. They are the same faces, meeting after meeting, day after day. You've got to give thought to the fact that the person you lay bare before friends and colleagues is the same person you'll be talking to tomorrow, and tomorrow, and tomorrow. And remember, every meeting is different. And the lineup on different subjects is different. If you make a fool of Bill in this meeting, you can count on his getting back at you just as soon as his chance for retribution comes along—probably when it hurts the most. There are some things you should play for the long haul. Use some of the techniques listed in this book to refute Bill's misinformation while holding on to his support.

Let him save face. It just makes good sense.

Follow the Persuasion Circle

Goethe, the German poet, novelist, and scientist, observed,

> "I can promise you to be honest, but I cannot promise you to be impartial."

There are very few people you'll meet in life who are truly impartial. Happily we all hold opinions. That's what makes life interesting. We hold them tenaciously, and because, as pointed out earlier in this book, the positions we hold are frequently tied closely to our psyche, family, fears, security, pride—these positions don't change easily. And that, very simply, is what this book is all about. How you can *change* people's opinions and have your point of view prevail.

But is this really possible? When you think how strongly ideas are held, and on such a deep, personal basis, is it really possible to change someone's mind?

Yes . . . and no.

It's possible to change the position a person holds on a subject, but not *all at once*. Let me tell you something that will be of great help to you in your efforts to persuade others—either in or out of the meeting. It's about how people change their minds.

People change their minds not by going directly from point A to point B. It's not that simple. They really travel around a circle from disbelief to belief. And how fast and how far they move around that circle depends on you—on how you present your persuasion, the kind of persuasion, and your understanding of how people think.

To understand the thinking pattern better I've developed this guide. I call it the "persuasion circle" and it looks like this:

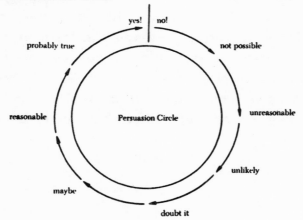

This is a diagram of the thinking process. What it says is that people's minds don't operate in a black-or-white fashion. They're not like computers that choose between YES and NO. The mind is much more complex, more subtle, more difficult to change categorically. The reason is simple; the human mind adds in many more elements than just facts. It adds such qualities as doubt, uncertainty, protection of self, anger, and many, many more. The persuasion circle shows that people go through a number of stages in moving from a NO to a YES position. They move through areas on their way to agreement. It doesn't happen all at one blow like turning on a light bulb. And if you expect it to, you're not only going to be disappointed, you can't be successful in your job of persuading others to see things as you do. Here are a few suggestions.

Understand that it takes time to change a person's mind. Understand the persuasion circle and how it works. Then you can learn to pace yourself as you try to move people over to your side of a subject.

Don't become impatient with others in the meeting. Remember, different individuals will hold to different points on the trip from NO to YES longer than others. Recognize this and try to tailor your persuasion to their timetable, not yours. It makes for a better climate. And more success.

Give them bits of persuasion to keep them moving. People move along the persuasion circle and must pass through the various points from disbelief to acceptance, so you must constantly give them enough fuel to move them from NO to YES. That's why you must develop *many* bits of support *before* you come to the meeting. There's a direct relationship between the amount of your preparation and the success you can achieve.

Mix your support information. Fact alone may not move a listener from one point in the circle to another. Use emotional arguments, "being part of the winning group," "the security of joining the team," "growth opportunities," etc. Man does not live by fact alone.

Expect stoppages. It's got to happen. Know they'll come as long as people are involved and be prepared to remove them . . . in good humor. Anger and frustration don't work.

Probe to define where the stoppage is and then honestly try to wipe it away. Remember, when

67

you persuade a single member, he'll help you persuade the rest.

Knowing about the persuasion circle should give you an important advantage over the others in the meeting. Just knowing the thinking pattern of the human mind gives you a chance to persuade more successfully. You go to a golf pro who explains why it's important to keep your head down when you swing. Or the tennis coach who points out why you must lift up on the ball to get it over the net. You apply their advice and are amazed that it works. This information on the persuasion circle works the same way. You "groove" your communication approach: know how people think, and use it to succeed in the meeting.

The rest is in your hands. *Don't* lift your head in the golf swing. *Don't* hit down on the ball in tennis. And *Don't* think people change their minds from black to white in one jump.

Don't forget the persuasion circle.

Don't Put Yourself in the "Zap" Position

Like practically everything in life, meetings are won or lost by the combined effect of small things. Small things that become BIG things when they're put together. If your opponents (and they're sitting all around you) are able to whittle away at your credibility, they will have successfully reduced your effectiveness and force—and the power of your ideas. One very subtle but deadly way is to lure you into the "zap" position.

And what exactly is the zap position? It's that position where you have opened yourself up for a quick karate chop that will stun you, make you look unsettled, unsure, as though you have shown bad judgment. Or it might make you look just plain foolish!

There are many, many zap positions, but here are some common examples.

1. When you get sucked out into an enthusiastic joyride. For instance:

> BILL: "And we could immediately commit for the packaging for the year. Then we'd be ahead of the entire market."

> YOU: "Great idea! No one could catch us then. The sooner the better!" (spoken enthusiastically).

> BILL: "On the other hand, that's a risky move. Not the best marketing judgment."

ZAP!!!

2. When you attempt to translate for someone who doesn't want to be translated. For instance:

> YOU: "What Jane is saying, I think, is that the swimming pool is more important to the town than the parking lot."
> JANE: "Wrong! What I mean is just the opposite."

ZAP!!!

3. When you report for someone else who wants to pull your cord. For instance:

> YOU: "Gene says he'll have no trouble meeting the date for the delivery of the cars."

70

GENE: "Wait a minute! I never said that! You must have misunderstood. That's ridiculous!"

ZAP!!!

4. When you allow yourself to become emotional on a subject, proving that your thinking is bound to be flaky. For instance:

SARAH: "I'm for waiting until the research is in. Then we'll be more sure of ourselves."

YOU: "Wait, wait, wait. Be sure! A little more sureness and we'll be out of business!"

SARAH: (Cooly) "I know we'd all like to indulge ourselves in emotion. But, unfortunately, this is a business and we're dealing with a lot of other people's money."

ZAP!!!

There are hundreds of other situations that can put you in the zap position. And when you're there, you're very vulnerable and your chance to win the meeting has been reduced to nil.

What can you do about it? Be smart and be careful.

Watch for the zappers. They're easy to spot. Every company has them. And when you isolate them, be extra careful not to fall into their trap.

71

Observe how they work and treat them accordingly.

Don't make statements that ask for acceptance or approval from others in the meeting. Don't openly ask someone to state that he agrees with you. You're buying trouble if you do. Sometimes if you know a person really well, you might decide to try it. But, frankly, it's rarely worth the risk. You can easily be sandbagged!

Stay with positive statements. Statements you know you can support. Statements that if challenged will put the burden of proof on the challenger.

Stay out of the emotional area. It's a bog! A miasma of mucky ground where you can easily sink in up to your neck. Business people, town boards, teacher/parent groups—everyone responds to speakers who walk on the side of logic. Emotion can be used effectively, but you must *know* how and when to use it. And why. Don't let emotion lead you into a zap trap.

Remember, zapping isn't the nicest of techniques. And certainly you don't want to get zapped. But if you find a chronic zapper, why not give it back to him?

ZAP!!!

72

There's Nothing New in theWorld

There are lots of good ways to get listeners to suspend their disbelief, to come over to your side and buy what you have been trying to prove. There's logic. There's fact. There're numbers. There's emotional appeal. There's having an authority speak on your side, supporting what you've said. But there's one bit of proof that's irresistible if you use it correctly and at the right time.

That's when you can show that what you want to do *now* has been done *before* . . . and with good results. If it's happened before, why shouldn't it happen again? If it's worked before, why not now? It's very difficult to say no to this kind of proof. The reason? Simple. You have brought the listener closer to reality. And the reality of success in the past will sweep away any lingering doubt. Let me give you an example.

You are in a meeting to discuss a new advertising campaign. You are proposing the use of a personality to present your message. The inevitable doubter says, "Personalities don't work in advertising."

Move in . . .

> "It's hard to support that point. Look what Henry Fonda has done for GAF. Or Bill Shattner for Promise Margarine. Or Wolfman Jack for Clearasil. Or Joe DiMaggio for Mr. Coffee."

Remember the opponent of your idea is now at a big disadvantage. He's challenged your position and you've given specific examples. Now the onus is on him to muster proof that you're wrong. And it isn't easy. You're on your way to winning the point.

Another example of how to use past happenings to prove the present—or the future: You're at a community board meeting. You're trying to gain support for a plan to get the youth of the town involved in political action. "Oh," says one of the doubting meeting members, "what can young people do? They're as helpless as the rest of us."

You move in . . .

"Helpless? Hardly! We should remember that the youth of the country practically single-handedly got McGovern the Democratic nomination. They were the movers who drove President Johnson out of office and stopped the only war the United States ever lost. And a small group, by passively invading a nuclear building site in New Hampshire, put the name 'Seabrook' in everyone's vocabulary."

It will be hard for your opponents to deny you your position.

Let's try another point. You are in a new product meeting and the subject of color comes up. It's been suggested that color is something you can worry about later. You don't agree. So you say so.

"The worst thing a marketer can do in today's market is to neglect thinking about the color of his product. I'm sure you've read about when all the cars on the road were black . . . and then color broke the automotive market wide open. Or when all bars of soap were white . . . and Camay first went to colors to match your

75

bathroom. And remember when there were only white sheets . . . and no others? And white-painted walls . . . and no other colors? We've got to look at color *now*, before someone else does and steals our market."

One final example. You're in a meeting on financial planning for the future. The meeting members are worried about the increasing cost of goods. They're worried enough not to want to go ahead with the introduction of the company's new moisturizing lotion product. You want to allay that fear. So you point out . . .

"Increasing cost of goods is a worry, but it's a worry that faces all marketers equally. If you were to ask a margarine manufacturer what he'd do if his cost of soybeans were to go from $3.25 to $12.00 a bushel, he'd tell you he'd go out of business. If you asked a baker what he'd do if wheat rose from $1.73 a bushel to $4.78, he'd shrug and laugh and tell you he'd close his doors. Or a banker, what would happen if the prime rate went up . . . say from 5½ percent to 10 percent, he'd tell you business would come to a dead stop. But all these things *happened!* And everybody is still in business. Let's worry about the cost of goods, but let's get the new product out there. And sell it!"

Everyone says look to the future. Here's a case where looking back will help you win the meeting.

Build Yourself an Image

How people see you is as critical in today's world as what you are. The communication media, radio, TV, newspapers, magazines have made this the age of the image. What we *know* about almost all famous people is colored by the way we *see* them.

Think about how we *see* some well-known people. Sam Ervin, former senator from North Carolina, superlative lawyer and legislator, culti- vates the image of a simple country lawyer. Why? Because the simple country boy has the heart of most Americans. And country boys who make good win public approval for their proposals.

Winston Churchill, one of the great men of our or any century, gave the appearance of a hard-drinking, shoot-from-the-hip rebel. Behind this façade was a precise mind, clear thinking, hard hitting. Why the image? Because Churchill knew the people of England needed a "bulldog" to lead a country in desperate trouble.

And they followed him to victory.

There are good examples in advertising of the use of an "image." Take Frank Perdue, the chicken man. Dull, straight, no inflection in his speech, no emotion. The image? A dull, straight man with no time for the social graces. Why? Because a dull, straight man like this spends *all* his time breeding the best of all possible chickens. And Lord help the people working for him if they don't follow his lead.

Or Catherine Deneuve, blonde and beautiful, looking out from the page of your favorite magazine. But she's more than beauty. She's the essence of control and sophistication; the spirit of today's woman, beautiful and independent. The "image" Chanel believes will sell its product to the men . . . and influence the women. No wonder such a high premium is placed on this lovely woman.

Early in your career, you should spend some time thinking of the image *you* wish to project in the meeting. The right image can be a powerful weapon. One that few people *ever* think about.

Obviously, you aren't going to take on an image, like Red Skelton in his tramp routine, Columbo—the TV detective—or John Wayne. But, there are images that can work for you as a member of a meeting group. Images that appeal to the listeners, make them want to listen to you, help them to believe. Here are a few image projections for you to think about:

1. People like people who put forth the image of being honest and fair. Listeners are universally united in this view. It is critical to project this image.

2. Listeners yearn for strong facts but rebel against anyone who comes off with the image of being pretentious or overbearing.

3. People are turned off by anyone who refuses to see other points of view. They admire strength, but not rigid bias.

4. Meeting members, in fact everybody, suspects the emotional speaker. The one who speaks too fast, jumps around in his thinking, shouts, etc. They distrust his judgment and usually rightly so. Remember, you can *appeal* to

the emotions, but you must control your emotional image.

5. On the other hand, listeners like security. Calm, well-directed control. Good reasoning has big power, particularly when presented in a firm, well-modulated voice. In a world of uncertainty, it's not surprising that listeners tend to follow the leader who offers sureness and stability.

6. All the world loves the innovator, the creative person. And a person who has the image of being creative has a good deal more freedom than others. So, the creative image is a good one. *But be careful.* If your listeners begin to doubt the rationality of your creative ideas, your ability to find unusual solutions, this image will turn around and bite you. Then you'll be put in the same class as the emotional speaker we talked about previously.

7. The obstructionist is disliked by almost everyone. We spend endless time in meetings—long, tough ones. There is no sympathy for the villain whose only contribution is to further extend your time in the meeting room.

8. As in any speaking situation, listeners dislike anyone who has earned the image of being a

80

nonstop talker, who goes on and on, saying nothing. This kind of speaker is so dull, he deserves the description Samuel Johnson gave to a speaker he was forced to listen to. Johnson said,

> "He is not only dull in himself, he is the cause of dullness in others."

Think about how you project yourself. Think about it and then set out to develop an image that will support what you have to say, that will make what you say have more effect, and bring about the changes you want.

Look to your image. It can definitely help you win the meeting.

Find the "Better Way"

Obviously, one of the surest ways to win the meeting is to solve a problem that's plaguing the meeting members, a problem no one else is able to solve. If you can do this, there's very little doubt that your contribution will be recognized and you'll see the meeting come out the way you wish.

But, there's one hitch. It's not always easy to solve a difficult problem. That's what meeting members struggle with every day. Let's examine the problem of solving problems.

It probably doesn't surprise you that most problems seem to lead to a limited number of possible solutions, most of them unsatisfactory. For instance, one of the ways to solve the traffic problem in New York City is to bar all cars from

82

Manhattan Island. But that would reduce the sales of all the businesses and put an impossible burden on public transportation. So it's a solution, but not an acceptable one. The solution we usually end up with is to urge people not to drive into the city—a solution that is hardly original.

Or, to reduce air pollution, we would stop burning coal and oil for fuel and use solar energy. Unfortunately, most of our plants would have to close down because solar energy is not yet ready to take up the slack. So, that isn't an acceptable solution. The solution we settle for is to give plants a number of years to put in smoke abatement equipment.

This situation of solutions that aren't really solutions is with us all the time. And particularly in the meeting. This is bad . . . but it's also good. It gives you a big chance to stand out from the rest. But, how? How do you come to better, more original solutions to problems? By using your brain, by making a *conscious* effort to be original, innovative, creative. And, most important, by knowing that original solutions *do* exist for most problems, if you direct your mind to search them out.

83

Let's roam outside the meeting room for some examples. For years the photographic industry has been plagued with one great problem, a problem that has kept people from taking more pictures, or kept them from taking any at all. Problem? You don't know what your picture will look like until days later. And when you do get them, there're all fuzzy . . . and besides, by then you're not as interested in looking at pictures.

The creative solution? Well, a man named Land solved this big problem by inventing the Polaroid camera. He solved the problem a different way. He had his camera develop your picture right before your eyes. That's what I mean by an *innovative* solution to a problem.

Another example. A number of years back the ocean liners discovered they weren't making money. The airlines had taken their business away. Lots of attempts were made to cut back on fuel, to reduce the number of staff on board, to search out new routes, to advertise the food, etc. No good. They still lost money. They were being forced out of business.

Then someone had a creative solution. Maybe, he asked, maybe we're not looking at the problem the right way. Maybe that's why we can't come up with a solution. Then he found it. The liners weren't in the travel business anymore. They couldn't compete with the airlines. *Now* they were in the resort business. People went on a ship to get away from something, not to *go* somewhere. They were in competition not with Pan Am, but with Grossinger's. And that's the way the liners are making money today. That's what I call an innovative solution to a problem.

One more example. Obviously, perishables such as milk, yogurt, and eggs present a problem of delivery. That's why you see those refrigerated trucks backed up to your supermarket every morning. Well, I remember one meeting I attended where a company was getting ready to put a perishable product into a test market to determine how well it would sell nationally. But there was one problem. How to deliver samples in the test city. No one wanted to buy trucks for that one city. Obviously, competition wouldn't help out and deliver a product that would be in competition with them. What to do? An innovative solution was needed. And it came along.

Someone suggested they go to the local milk company (they were still delivering milk to the door then) and ask them to place the product for the company. They asked the company . . . and the company delivered directly to the people. Another creative solution to a difficult problem. A solution that solved a tough problem in a different way.

Next time you're in an important meeting, stop for a moment and *think*. Don't always be drawn to the usual solution. In fact, don't *accept* the usual solution . . . if a creative one's possible. Examine the problem. Turn up your innovative juices. Force your mind out of ordinary channels and develop a *really* creative idea.

The rewards for this kind of thinking are big. People always remember innovative, bright solutions to problems that plague them. And, most important, they remember the person who presents them. It's an excellent path to winning the meeting!

Avoid the Meeting
That's Doomed to Fail

Early on in your career you've got to learn to recognize the meeting that is held too soon, with the wrong people to solve the problem, with materials that still only exist in the heads of the few members of the group. Any of these are a *sure* path to failure and will require several *more* meetings just to get even again. A combination of the three is disaster! A meeting called on this basis is a complete misuse of the communications system.

Here are the ingredients of meeting failure. A meeting is called to discuss the introduction of a new cosmetic product that will offer consumers the latest fashion look plus skin moisturizing if they have a dry skin condition. The product is the first item on the agenda.

Unfortunately, R&D hasn't yet completed the testing, so there's no way to know whether the product will work as planned.

Unfortunately, the consumer research is still in the field, so there's no way to measure the interest the consumer might have in such a product.

And the lawyers haven't completed the name search, so you don't know if you have a name or not.

There's not much to talk about. It's a "Too Soon" meeting.

Well, you suggest, perhaps it would be a good idea to discuss the package copy that has been developed.

Unfortunately, the package designer isn't at the meeting, so you can't find out if the copy will fit the package space. In lieu of the package designer, the R&D chemist decides to comment on the copy. Of course, he has no experience or knowledge in this area, but he's there! He doesn't like the approach of the copy. Thinks the words are wrong . . . the type too light . . . maybe the headline should say "beauty" more . . . etc.

You're in trouble. Deep trouble! One thing you can be sure of in the meeting: If you have the "wrong," people there, they'll say the wrong things. Unproductive things. Things that complicate, not solve.

Ah, but the advertising. We could talk about the advertising, you say in desperation. Okay, let's talk about the advertising. After all, the copywriter *is* in the meeting.

"Now," says the copywriter, leaning forward, "the copy isn't *really* ready. I mean, it's being worked on, but you'll have to *imagine* what it will be like when it really is finished. Oh, we don't have any pictures yet, but I'm thinking about a girl . . . probably about the age of sixteen. She may be standing outside . . . or she *could* be inside . . . well, I haven't really made up my mind yet. . . ."

Very, very few people have the kind of mind that lets them *imagine* what something such as copy is going to be like. Most everyone brought up in the business world is taught to be very specific about very specific subjects. They can't just turn that off. If your copy ever gets out of that meeting without being damaged beyond repair, it will be a miracle. The "Imagine-What-It-Will-Be-Like" direction is a collision course with disaster in the meeting.

89

For your own salvation, don't *ever* be responsible for a "Too Soon," "Wrong People," "Imagine-What-It-Will-Be-Like" meeting. Anyone who lets himself get into this situation deserves no sympathy. In fact, if you can, don't even attend such a meeting. If pressed, suggest a delay.

One thing *is* certain. This kind of meeting you'll never win.

The Victim of Secondhand Information

Here's a problem that may be the greatest meeting time waster of all! You've been in this meeting, but you may not have analyzed what was happening, why your meeting was bound to fail from the beginning.

The meeting is discussing the building of an extension on the town library—a new reading room. You've taken the strong position that this is something long overdue, that the costs of an extension are far less than the building of a new building somewhere nearby. But then someone pipes up.

> "The architect says that the ground is too soft to build an extension there."

Your position has suffered a major setback. After all, he *is* the authority. Without his support you couldn't possibly win. But you ask logically:

> "I'd like to discuss this problem with the architect. Is he here?"
>
> "No. The architect couldn't attend. But he said . . ."

There is no way this question can now be solved; there's no way around the impasse. You can't win. You're the victim of secondhand information.

Five months later, after several more meetings, the architect *is* available and under questioning says:

> "Oh, I *never* said the ground was too soft. I said the ground was too soft in April to *start* building then. Of course, in June the ground is plenty firm enough. . . ."

The report of the little man who wasn't there is a costly translation!

Another example. You're discussing putting a new chemical in your company's laundry detergent, a chemical that will give you a cleaning advantage over your competition. An important marketing plus!

92

"But [says one of the chemists from R&D] we've been talking to one of our lawyers who has been following the Washington committees, the FDA in fact, and he says that there's a good chance they'll find this chemical unacceptable for general use."

"Unacceptable?"

"Yes, unacceptable."

Your support of the new ingredient is severely weakened. Of course, you could ask the lawyer directly, but he isn't there. The meeting must come to a close ... and reconvene probably several more times.

When you finally get the lawyer into a meeting, you find he *really* said something quite different. Yes, he said the FDA was looking at the chemical. But they were really worried about its use in something you put into your mouth, like toothpaste, not laundry products.

You have been cut down by the secondhand-information carrier. All you can hope for is that the forward motion of the new laundry project is not stalled beyond repair.

Don't accept secondhand information on important points. If you think there could be a problem in the meeting, *insist* the authority be present. There's just too much variation in what *is* said and what secondhand-information carriers *think* is said.

You remember the game we all used to play as kids. We called it Gossip. It was played this way: Someone would whisper something in the ear of the person next to him. She would pass it on to the next person . . . and so on. By the time it got around to the end of the line of people, the idea was *completely* different from what was originally said. And everyone had a good laugh.

Not so in the meeting. There's many a slip twixt the cup and the lip, as the saying goes. Be careful. People who report what *other* people say are open to all kinds of misinterpretation and misrepresentation—not necessarily intentional. But misrepresentation is a costly situation when you're trying to solve problems.

Don't let the secondhand-information genie wipe out your chance of winning the meeting.

Psychological Pressures That Work

Winning the meeting is simply a system of applying pressures to make your points of view prevail. Pressures can be logical; like reason, fact, or numbers. But there is an equally powerful force present in all human communications. The force of psychological pressure. Pressures that raise doubts in the mind of the individual meeting member. Pressures that make the individual ask himself if he is doing the right thing . . . voting the right way . . . moving with the right tide. You should learn to use these psychological weapons because they can exert forces that frequently out-gun the logical. But first you must learn to recognize these forces, recognize how they work, and how to apply them.

Earlier in this book we talked of the two roles everyone in a company or a group plays. The role of the company and its needs, and the role of the individual and his personal rewards. The psychological pressures I'm going to tell you about apply to the latter. Remember that everyone is concerned about the image he presents to the group. It doesn't take a psychiatrist to prove to you that the image people hold of you is of critical importance to you. Probably equal in weight to your job . . . your family . . . your future. The "me" in the individual is gigantic. And it's here that the doubts can grow.

I assume that by now you are aware that the meeting is hardly ever a place for the democratic trading of ideas. The objective of most meetings you'll attend is to make your point of view prevail. You'll want to win! One way to do this is to weaken your opponents and their points of view. If you're perceptive, you can do this extremely well by the use of psychological pressures. Such as these.

The Meeting Before the Meeting

Here is a technique I've seen work with great effectiveness. Some morning you're going to have a meeting on an important subject. There's a good deal of uncertainty about which way the boss is thinking. Is he for the idea or against it? Does he have a slightly different solution?

The morning before the meeting you work out a way to meet with him—on another subject, of course. But the other members of the projected meeting know of your earlier one. If asked what you talked to the boss about, you are cryptic, evasive. "Oh nothing in particular, I just wanted to touch base with him on a few things."

You'll be amazed at the psychological effect this can have. When the meeting takes place, the waverers will be tentative, uncertain. The fence sitters will tend to follow your leads. Your opponents will probably hold back—perhaps enough for you to gain an advantage. It's an interesting technique. Try it.

The Categorical Statement

People generally avoid confrontations. They find them unpleasant. They also find it easier to slip around a subject. Most people are noncombative, perhaps because it allows them to shift positions more easily. The same applies to the meeting and the way meeting members act. Someone says something they disagree with and their answer is usually "Well, that's possible, but it could be that . . .," etc. A gentle denial. A nonconfrontive answer. This leaves a big opportunity for you if you want to put an opponent on the psychological defensive. Use the Categorical Statement:

OPPONENT: "Our share has been going down in Cleveland."

YOU: "WRONG!" (No qualification. No evasion. No gentlemanly approach.)

Or . . .

OPPONENT: "I know Bill will agree with me."

YOU: "No—I don't agree!" (Smile)

You'll be amazed at how this directness will

topple even strong personalities. Put someone on the defensive, and put yourself in the leadership role.

If used correctly, it can be a very effective psychological weapon. One obvious warning. Be sure you're right.

The Past-Failure Reminder

Everyone has had a past failure, something he'd rather not remember or have called to public attention. Like the stock you recommended to all your friends that went down to $1 a share. Or the lawyer you supported enthusiastically for councilman who was convicted of fraud. Or the drop you predicted in property taxes based on inside information, only to have them go up 125 percent. Everyone has some of these.

Now remember that before the meeting you're going to try to gain a psychological edge over one of your opponents, an edge that will make the others in the meeting doubtful as to his judgment. You can't knock him out of the meeting at this point, but you can tarnish his contributions.

99

Here's another way to use psychological pressure.

> "Bill, this idea sounds like those dried seeds you were going to use as premiums last year. You must still have a warehouse full of them, don't you?" (You know he does.)

With everyone listening, you have just taken a bit of the luster off whatever he might be supporting. Not a knockout blow . . . but telling. If a person can make a boo-boo like that and end up with so many seeds, his judgment is . . . well?

Or . . .

> "Mary, you were always one to push that new math. Remember how you fought to have it installed in our school? Well, I just saw an article by the heads of math at Harvard, Yale, and Columbia saying that the worst thing that could have happened in American education was to go to that system. The kids now can't do simple arithmetic. We're not going to face another problem like that, I hope."

"What You Said a While Back" Recall

There was one psychological pressure technique I saw used most effectively several years back. It

100

took the receiver right off balance for the rest of the meeting. As the discussion developed, it was obvious that a conflict circled around two of the meeting members. They dueled with each other, each giving and taking for about three-quarters of an hour. The other members came in occasionally, but always the battle was back in the two members' hands. Suddenly, one of them changed tone and said,

> "You know, that idea Jim suggested just a while ago was an interesting one. Jim, would you mind repeating it again? It's worth repeating."

Poor Jim. He couldn't remember what he had suggested. At the request all eyes turned directly to him and threw him completely off. He fumbled and hawed and mumbled. His mind was as flat as a punctured tire. He never got back into the discussion again. The psychological pressure had taken him out of the game.

The "Faint Praise" Ploy

Think of the meeting as a blackboard that is wiped clean when the meeting begins. From that point on, everything that's said or done is recorded and the sum of all points has a dramatic effect on which way the meeting goes, which way the decisions are made. Anything that you can do to weaken your opponent's position is something that will work in your favor. It will help you win the meeting.

One of the most effective techniques I've seen used is what I call the "faint praise" approach. It works like this. Someone in the meeting is holding forth strongly on a point, pressing hard, detailing and supporting the position taken. You listen with a straight face, no emotion showing. When the person is finished and obviously waiting for a response, you look at that person and make a comment that refuses to give any value to what's been said. It's as if you want to go past the point made to something of more substance. As if you were embarrassed. You could respond with an unemotional . . .

> "Interesting." [Period. And then turning away from the speaker] "I wonder if the time hasn't come for us to look at another approach."

Another good response (notice they're totally non-committal) would be:

102

"I'm sure that's true." (Silence.)

or

"An original thought." (And again you turn away to another point.)

Or, one that's used effectively by one of my British friends, simply,

"Quite."

The polite but cold disregard is difficult to deal with. It will be noticed by the other members around the table. The person subjected to the "faint praise" usually finds it hard to handle and you will have gained a psychological edge.

There are literally hundreds of psychological techniques you can learn to use in the meeting situation. They're all aimed at giving you an "up" on those who wish to see your point of view fail. Think about the use of these weapons. Jot them down as you see them used. Recognizing them is an important first step.

Using them can help you win the meeting.

Isolate the Big Point
That Will Win

"There is no adequate defense, except stupidity,
against the impact of a new idea."
—Percy W. Bridgman

I've found that while scores of ideas cross the table,
there is always *one* point that proves critical to
winning the meeting—a point, unfortunately, that
becomes obvious to everyone *in* the meeting—at a
time when most meeting members don't have the
information to exploit it. I've seen it happen
hundreds and hundreds of times. And I've always
said, "What a big win for someone . . . if he'd
looked ahead and isolated that one question and
had come to the meeting with the answer in his
pocket."

With the information to confront that Big Point,

the whole meeting could tumble all the way to your camp. Without it, too bad. You'll need another meeting. Or several.

Probably no one will argue with the idea that *one* point can be all important in the meeting. That it can determine which way the decision goes. The real problem is how can you determine beforehand what that point will be? Isolating the point is doubly difficult because the *one* point that can win the meeting is more often than not, not the main idea being discussed.

How then do we find this elusive keystone point? There are a number of places to look.

Look at the company's present position. Too many meeting members think of the meeting as isolated from the company world around them. Not true. Think of the meeting as what it is—a piece of the company's total business thrust. Just one activity in many going on at the same time. Why is this important? Because if you think this way, you'll have a better chance of finding that "Big Point" idea to win the meeting.

For instance, if the company's last quarter's earnings were down and the president has expressed dis-

105

satisfaction with this performance, the big point may be profit. See how *your* meeting position fits into the profit picture. You may have found the idea that will make you win. Or, perhaps your chairman has just made a speech to the American Marketing Association condemning animated commercials. Can you defend their use in your present marketing plan? It's just the point to bring you down.

Think ahead.

Check back on problems. If, for instance, the boss thinks the sales force can't handle any more new products (they're too busy), and you are recommending a new product, it could be the end of your position. Not that your idea is bad, but at this moment the boss is deeply concerned with the work load on the sales force. He may let your new product recommendation go by. *But* if you thought about his concern, *and* came to the meeting with the Big Point solution—perhaps of using an outside sales force— you could have won the day.

Look into the history of your organization. Later on we talk about your efforts to convince the town board to set up a daycare center. In that example checking back revealed that an earlier daycare center had been involved in a kidnapping attempt. Look back into history *before* you come to the meeting. To be forewarned is to be forearmed. If you know something about the history of an organization, you may be able to come to the meeting with the Big Point solution that will enable you to have your point of view prevail.

For instance, if you're lobbying for a town manager, and you know that the town's last one, years ago, walked off with a bundle of money, you've got deep trouble. But, you *can* come to the meeting with an armful of evidence to prove that *hundreds* of towns are on this sytem with *good*, honest managers. And besides, you have a check system that will never let what happened before happen again. But, if you go in unprepared . . . you'll be dead.

Be conscious of the problem of breaking new ground. Often we go to meetings with the mistaken idea that the human being is a logical thinker. Not so. Our logic is inhibited by literally hundreds of complex emotions, emotions that are intimate and often subconscious. And though they're very personal, they're also broadly held. One of these deep-seated emotions is the fear of the unknown, the fear of treading on ground you haven't walked before, the fear of extending yourself into an unknown area. Those of you who remember your Shakespeare will recall Hamlet's statement that the unknown

> ".... makes us rather bear those ills we have
> Than fly to others that we know not of.
> Thus conscience does make cowards of us all. ...."

And don't be misled. This fear doesn't only exist in philosophy, it's right beside you in the meeting room. If you're urging your shampoo company to go into the hair dryer field (something completely new to them) . . . think about the "know not of" fear.

If you're trying to persuade your local sports club to admit women members . . . think about the "know not of" fear.

If you're suggesting a *new* way to register voters to your local election board . . . think about the "know not of" fear.

Of course, these fears can be overcome, sometimes easily, *if* you've identified them early—before the meeting—and have brought

108

persuasive facts to destroy them. Without these facts, your chances of success are limited.

In every meeting there's *one* important point, one "keystone idea" that will tip the balance between acceptance and rejection. It's always there, waiting to jump up and bring the meeting to a grinding halt. Most people who go to meetings have never taken this close a look at the things that make meetings fail . . . or succeed. If you spend a little time looking for the Big Point, your success average in the meeting will improve considerably. And half the battle is won by knowing what to look for.

Before you go into your next meeting, look for that *one* idea that must be solved before you can get the company movers to agree with your point of view. It'll be time well spent. It will increase your success rate substantially.

The Peter Lorres
of the Meeting Table

You remember (and if you don't, you should) the marvelously devious characters Peter Lorre used to play in movies like *A Coffin for Demetrius* and *The Maltese Falcon.* Slippery, shifty, cunning characters, always with a hidden motive, eternally pursuing a personal gain. I don't mean to shock you, but the same kind of characters people the chairs around the meeting table, and they pursue the same "dark" objectives. They don't smoke long Turkish cigarettes, sidle into seamy hotels in the dead of night, and carry black Lugers with silencers. But, like the Lorre characters, they *do* have hidden motives and they can act with amazing duplicity. They are the professional villains of the meeting table.

110

These types are many and varied. But you must get to know them. You will have to recognize their style and learn to deal with them. Here are a few common ones.

The Deliberate Misunderstander

He's a very common type, usually found singly in most meeting rooms. He often wears a worried expression, as though troubled by something he always finds difficult to explain. He usually makes such statements as "I just can't understand how we could have overlooked that possibility." Or, after a thorough explanation is given, repeats the same call, "I just don't understand . . .," etc. This bird is easy to identify because no matter how many times a subject is explained, he will always respond with "I just don't know how . . .," etc.

The deliberate misunderstander is a hard one to deal with because he will always come back to second-guess you. That's his tactic. If you can make him part of a decision, you might defuse him. But this is unlikely. One positive thing is that after hearing this deliberate misunderstander a number of times, the meeting members often neutralize him by disregarding his worries. He is a much greater problem if he's a person of power who can't be ignored. Then you just have to tough it out and hope enough members of the meeting will say, "Let's move on."

The Combatant

This fellow comes to the meeting with all chambers loaded with live ammunition. He looks upon the meeting as a place to rid himself of anger and frustration. The moment the battle is joined, the salvos fly. He will attack anyone. The subject soon becomes secondary to the "fight." He thunders and volleys. Logic and reason be damned. And once he says something, there's no chance he'll change. He fits Winston Churchill's definition of a fanatic.

> "A fanatic is one who can't change his mind and won't change the subject."

Luckily this fellow is not all that difficult to deal with. Logic can destroy his credibility but not shut him up. Sometimes this type will frighten other members so they hold back rather than risk his attack. That's not the right approach. Go right after him if he's wrong. But remember one thing: He is most vulnerable to logic and calm. That's your weapon. Calm. Keep cool and you'll soon cage this terrible tiger.

The Fellow Behind the Water Cooler

He's not really behind the water cooler, but he might just as well be. If he isn't hidden physically, he is verbally. He's the fellow who sits quietly all through the meeting, not disagreeing . . . or agreeing, for that matter. You have every right to presume that since he doesn't put in a point of view, he agrees with what you've been saying.

Wrong!

For that's the MO of this villain. A quiet type, he doesn't want to make the effort to push his points; it offends his meek manner. But, be careful, he's far more dangerous than he appears. Here's the way he works his dastardly acts!

You finish up the meeting and it appears that you've managed to bring about an acceptance of your point of view. You're feeling pretty good. You've been working to get agreement for a long time. Walking down the hall with one of the meeting members, you comment on how the project will move ahead rapidly now. Finally.

Behind you in the hall is the Fellow-Behind-The-Water Cooler. He looks unhappy, shaking his head. Then he utters the words that he *should* have said in the meeting!

> "You know, I can't go along with that idea. I just can't support that way of going."

POW! Another meeting!

This fellow is found in *all* companies. He is as destructive as a company strike because he's always there to bring you back again and again to the meeting room. You've got to label him and learn to disarm him. For your own good . . . and for the company. How do you handle a fellow like this? It's really quite simple. Don't let him out of the room without a verbal commitment. But be careful, this fellow is slippery. He'll do anything to avoid being pinned down. Don't let him get away! Once you've identified him, ask the question directly:

> "John, how about you? You have anything to add?"

> "No. Not really. Only . . . well, it's not important."

114

"Oh yes it is. *Do* you have a problem? If you do, let's have it."

"I guess it'll work . . ."

"*Do* you support the agreement?"

"Oh, all right. I support it."

"Thank you."

Be persistent. If you're not, it will cost you dearly in effort and time.

The Selective Listener

If you're looking for a specialist, you've found one in the Selective Listener. His whole communication system is refined only to hear what he wants to hear. And to reinforce this, he will respond only to those triggers that support his strictly enforced bias. Try as you may, this villain will only rise to ideas he came to the meeting with. In fact, he's probably been coming into meetings for years with the same premises. For instance:

MEETING MEMBER: "I propose we go to the town board and present our plans for the school running track. If they can vote for more taxes, we

115

should be able to get them to put aside enough money for our project.

SELECTIVE LISTENER: "Taxes! Yes, they certainly vote more taxes! Every year, in fact."

MEETING MEMBER: "Are you against the school running track?"

SELECTIVE LISTENER: "I've heard that the taxes in Greenwich are lower than ours here. Can you imagine that?"

MEETING MEMBER: "But can we expect you to support our motion?"

SELECTIVE LISTENER: "We really should take a stand on taxes . . ."

Fortunately, the Selective Listener eventually focuses himself out of the meeting process in most companies. The members themselves, however, must often suffer a long time as he fumbles in the candy jar for his own particular sweet.

The best way to combat the Selective Listener is to recognize him. Don't turn to him and expect any help in pushing the meeting forward. The Selective Listener is Draculalike in that he lives on the thinking of others and contributes none of his own.

116

The Quick Solution Finder

This is the way this invidious fellow surfaces. IM-
MEDIATELY. This Peter Lorre of the meeting table is,
above all, quick. He doesn't let fact or reason or
logic get in his way. He goes right to the throat of
the problem . . . and is invariably wrong! He's the
living example of the saying that,

> "There's no problem in the world for which
> there isn't a quick . . . and wrong solution."

You'll usually find this fellow in every group.
Someone may say:

> "There must be a reason why we're not selling
> in Chicago."

His response is:

> "They can't pronounce the name of the product.
> That's why."

Wham! Just like that. You're taken aback for the moment by the swiftness—and superficiality—of the
answer. But it doesn't bother the Quick Solution

117

villain. That's his way of thinking and you can't stop him.

How to handle this character? There's really little you have to worry about with this fellow. He has self-destruct built into himself. Just remember not to get involved in his "superrapid," flaky thinking. It'll just frustrate you. Chances are that no one in the room will pay too much attention to him anyway. And there's no cure. He'll be back with another off-target idea in the next meeting. Another idea that'll leave the listeners shaking their heads.

There are many, many villains of the meeting table. Most you can't change; you just have to live with them. What you *can* do is understand how they work and learn how to avoid their traps.

It'll help you win the meeting.

Strike at the Right Time

Winston Churchill once said,

"In one respect a cavalry charge is very like ordinary life. So long as you are all right, firmly in your saddle, your horse in hand, and well armed, lots of enemies will give you a wide berth. But as soon as you have lost a stirrup, have a rein cut, have dropped your weapon, are wounded or your horse is wounded, then is the moment when from all quarters enemies rush upon you."

The time you strike in battle is critical. I suggest the same is true in the meeting.

Timing is very sensitive when you sit around the table, when you plan to have your ideas accepted over all the others presented by your colleagues and opponents. The *timing* you use to present your idea, the *time* you choose to give your supporting proof, the *time* you decide to give your solution is critical. It can determine whether your idea (good or bad) is accepted warmly or thrown aside with disdain.

For example, let's say that early in the meeting you recommend that the solution to the town's financial problems is better administration. You suggest, "The mayor should be replaced with a board of three businessmen and women; people whose experience has proven they know how to handle a heavy work load and control the taxpayer's money." You're abruptly brushed aside.

Problem? The meeting members may feel the solution is coming to soon. Wrong *timing*.

Another example. You decide to propose a town art show to raise money needed for the church tower. You argue hard for your suggestion. You know it's a good idea and you believe in it. You're quickly voted down.

The meeting members probably don't fully understand the problem. Wrong *timing*.

And one last example. You want the condominium board members to authorize a plan to put on more security police for greater safety in the area. And you want them to pay for it! You push hard on your proposal. No, they say.

As simple as that. No! The people present feel too pressured. Overpowered. Wrong *timing*.

Let's assume all the foregoing ideas are good ones. Then why the rejection? They were badly timed. The people weren't ready for the proposals. Or they didn't fully understand the background of the problem. Or they were ready for the proposals, but not at that particular moment in the meeting. Or they felt rushed—pushed to a decision. That's why the ideas were turned down.

Think about it this way. Life has a pattern—timing. When you awake in the morning, you do things in a set pattern. You get up and start the coffee. You shower, dress, drink your coffee, put on your coat, lock the apartment door, go down the elevator, and catch the bus. All in that order. And you probably never change the sequence; it's always the same. Because people like things in a known order. If you move too fast, or too slow, or change too much, people get confused. Think what happens when you move to a cottage for the summer. Everything gets lost, you forget things, lose the car keys, forget to turn the kitchen light off—all because the sequence of actions and place has been changed.

The meeting is the same. Meetings have a beginning, middle, and an end—a sequence, a timing. And when they don't move through these patterns, the people involved get confused. And when they get confused, they vote no! That's why the ideas just discussed were voted down. Because their presentation was badly timed. A basic structure of human thinking was being violated.

Let me tell you something about the "time pattern" of the meeting. All meetings (and human logic) go through a number of steps from problem to solution. These are not artificial steps. They're not time-wasting, procrastinating steps. They're not pedantic, schoolmaster steps. They are, in fact, the most direct track to answering the problem at hand and bringing the meeting to a successful conclusion. They are the time pattern through which the thinking of the group must pass on the way to a solution. If you break this time pattern, you risk losing the meeting. And what is worse, coming up with the wrong solution. And both mean more meetings.

122

Here's how the time pattern of the meeting tracks the flow of logical thinking:

1. Do we know the problem?
2. How did it get to be a problem?
3. What are we trying to do?
4. How can we solve it?
5. What's the best way?
6. Let's go!

Let's go over each step and see how you can lead the members of the meeting from problem to solution, from disbelief to belief, from confusion to certainty. We'll go over these steps quickly, but don't underestimate their importance. In the meeting, be sure each is answered sufficiently. Without a full airing, it's almost impossible for you to get your point of view accepted.

Step 1: Do we know the problem? Review the problem under discussion. How big is it *really*? Is it smaller than everyone thinks? Is it complex or simple? Is it permanent or will it go away soon (like the snow on the streets)? Will it happen again? Just generally *feel* the problem all over.

123

Step 2: How did it get to be a problem? Where did it come from? What brought it into being (and if these were removed, would it stop being a problem—like rain will reduce the water shortage)? What are the expected effects of the problem? (No solutions yet, please.)

Step 3: What are we trying to do? Where do we want to come out? What would it be like if the problem didn't exist? Is there a complete solution? (Don't give it yet.) A partial solution? A compromise? Where *exactly* does the group want to come out?

Step 4: How can we solve it? This is the whole purpose of the meeting, of course. Look at *all* solutions suggested. Discuss them, or they'll be retalked in the hall later. And another meeting will be needed. What are the drawbacks of each solution? The advantages. Restate what you are trying to accomplish. Are the different solutions in conflict?

Step 5: What's the best way? Here's where a good deal of talking, arguing, persuading, selling, convincing, all come into play. Here's where you put the pressure behind *your* solution. Load it up with facts, reason, emotional support, etc. All the fuel that will bring the listeners all the way around the persuasion circle from NO to YES.

124

Step 6: Let's go! At this point, your solution should have been accepted. Only one thing remains: to make it as simple as possible to put into effect. Warning. This can be a dangerous point in the meeting. If your solution seems difficult to apply, the meeting can come apart. Your solution questioned again. Be careful. When you prepare the facts and support for your position, be sure you think about *how* you will put it into effect. Then you can put to bed any difficulties that arise at this point.

For instance, someone may say that manufacturing couldn't possibly handle your solution. *But* you've already talked to manufacturing and can report that they'd have *no* problem.

The time pattern of the meeting has been completed.

If you expect to win the meeting, you must realize that there *is* a pattern to thinking. Solutions given too soon (or too late) have little chance of being accepted. And someone else's solution will be bought. Or another meeting will be needed.

Be sure to strike at the right time.

The "Not Made Here" Syndrome

Except for true masochists, most of us soon find it impractical to try to run through stone walls—like the early professional football great Bronco Nagurski, who in one game plunged over the goal line and straight into the goalpost. When interviewed, he stated it was "the toughest guy I ever hit."

Now, there's a wall you can find in every company. That wall is the wall of "Not Made Here." It'll stop you dead in your tracks unless you learn to recognize it—and more importantly—how to cope with it.

Let's take a look at the Not Made Here problem and how it can affect you in the meeting. Imagine this meeting in progress.

An idea is being presented to R&D suggesting that a product formula used by the company in England might be adopted for products here. It could save at least two years of development time and a great deal of money. The company R&D representative jumps in to list *all* the reasons why it's a bad idea. A terrible idea! Real reason?

Not Made Here!

At a meeting of the high school teachers, you propose that the school examine a new reading technique that has been used with great success in Boston. "No," goes the cry of anguish. Reason?

Not Made Here!

You suggest a new consumer research technique that could shorten the time needed to complete a project. Research jumps in with all the reasons why not.

Not Made Here!

This problem of the ownership of an idea is obviously very close to the heart of most individuals. And the reason is simple if you think about it. By accepting an idea from outside, many people feel that it automatically reflects on their ability; that it will be thought that they should have come up with it themselves. On this basis, of

127

course, we would have to reinvent the steamboat and electric light over and over.

It's a touchy problem, but an important one. Because it can stop the acceptance of ideas in a group or organization and put you far behind your competition.

Well, what can be done about it? Not much, frontally. But a smart meeting member can use some techniques to open the door to good ideas. For instance, it's more often than not useless to try to fight the Not Made Here syndrome straight on. Minds harden. Tempers flare. Resistance stiffens. Remember how people feel about having to be *helped* to solve a problem.

Try the "infiltration" approach. Talk to R&D or Research or the teachers' representative *before* the meeting and see if you can work out a deal so *they* would gain stature from your suggestion. Work out the agreement beforehand. Then the meeting will go your way smoothly.

Another good approach is to get the "hang-back" department representative himself to make the suggestion in the meeting. Point out that this will show that he is keeping abreast of the times, keeping up with the newest ideas—then the new idea will have no stigma attached.

If *you* present the idea from outside, be sure you do it diplomatically. For instance:

> "I'm referring to the reading technique being used in the Boston schools. I'm sure Jim [teachers' representative] knows all about it and has studied it long before I came upon it. Jim is far more up to date on these things than I am."

Chances are that Jim will take the credit and praise and come along with you.

Finally, you can try to shoehorn the outside idea into something that is being done "at home." If it's packaging, you might try an approach like this:

> "This new stretch packaging technique looks like a good idea. In fact it seems to me, Betsy [packaging] has been working on that idea long before Green Giant started using it. Betsy should be getting a royalty from Green Giant."

Everyone will laugh, no criticism can be felt. And Betsy will likely want to fall into line and expound on *her* idea.

No question, the Not Made Here syndrome can

stop a company and a meeting dead in its tracks. If you know why this block occurs, you can work to break the barrier. Clearing away this stoppage can be a real accomplishment and will make you look good in the meeting. The meeting you're determined to win.

Try the Buddy System

The human being is a complex creature, in kind as well as physical makeup. He is put together not only of extremely subtle and interrelated organs, he's also made up of subtle and deep-seated patterns of thinking. In this brief chapter I'd like to deal with one of those patterns. The pattern of *labeling*.

What do I mean by labeling? Just that it is a common habit of people to typecast other people, to give each person they contact a character that colors whatever they say or propose. The same proposal to build a playground made by Dr. Spock and Richard Nixon will be viewed differently—even if the motivation is the same.

I've seen it happen hundreds of times when a

perfectly acceptable idea couldn't be sold because of the image the group held of the person proposing it. If the person was thought of as too liberal, the proposal was considered too liberal. Or they thought the person was not one to analyze a subject sufficiently; therefore the proposal wasn't thought out carefully. Or the person was flighty and, of course, the proposal was flighty.

This isn't an unusual situation. I know of a number of fashion designers who have the image of being "creative" and can sell "far out" creative ideas that other more conservative designers couldn't possibly sell to the same client. A lot is in the eye of the beholder.

Without question, we are all seen slightly differently from the way we might wish. Let's suppose you're seen as moving too quickly to a conclusion, or not being careful enough with the company's money, or any of a dozen other perceptions. What can you do about it? Or is it possible for you to do anything about it?

First of all, I urge you to examine the way others may see you—in your organization, group, or company. Chat with close friends, prod them to level with you. Then go to work to correct that image if it seems harmful to you. It can inhibit your growth for years if you don't spend some time thinking about it early on. But here's something else you can do to win your point at the meeting if that labeling exists.

Find a buddy in the meeting—someone who believes as you do and is going to present the same idea. Let him carry the ball. Let him make the presentation of the idea. Let him support his position with facts and reason. Then watch for the opportunity to move in and support his point of view. Not so openly that the idea becomes *your* position. It must remain his. Be like a sheepdog, gathering in all the support from the group you can to help his cause. Make statements of support that will improve *his* image, such as:

> "What Bill says makes a lot of sense to me. I never thought of it that way. Bill, what else do you think would help make your idea work?"

Every time you help Bill you help your position. But you haven't tainted the proposal with your overt presentation of it. Gradually, if the meeting group comes around to supporting the idea, you can just sit back and enjoy your success. You have made that success possible behind the scenes.

133

How to Win the Meeting

We've all heard people say,

"Well, another meeting. Walter will be beating the drum for spending more money, as usual."

If you're Walter, and you carry the label of being casual with money, you may have to resort to the buddy system to get your proposal passed.

Search Out
the Company Skeletons

A major problem in life for each of us is putting things in the right order of importance. There are all those situations that demand our attention—family, job, money, ideals, tennis, antique shopping, and literally hundreds of others. Life is a sorting machine that demands you put things in order and you are the sorter. You must remember, too, that everyone sorts differently, sets different values on individual issues.

If you get all the subjects in your life ranked correctly, according to importance, the world will say you're mentally well balanced. If you don't, if you misread the importance of something in your life—or your group or job or company—you're in trouble. Let's look at this quicksand of shifting values and how it operates.

You're in a meeting discussing a child's daycare center for your town. You're deeply committed because you believe in the project and think (obviously) that everyone must share your enthusiasm. The discussion gets more and more heated and hopelessly deadlocked. The more resistance you sense, the more you push and pressure the group. But you get nowhere. Nowhere!

Why? The skeleton . . .

If you had done your homework thoroughly, you'd have found that the town *did* have a daycare center a few years back . . . and a terrible thing happened. A child was kidnapped and held for several days before she was returned. The publicity cost the mayor his job and the town was sued for thousands of dollars. A big, bad memory still exists, even though no one speaks about it openly.

The "importance value" of the center is, of course, seen differently by the meeting members than by you. Where you assumed it to be a plus for the town, they saw it as a big problem. A bad, bad memory. The skeleton did you in. You never really had a chance. And you should have known it.

Or, you're in a meeting discussing a new beauty aid product you've been pushing to introduce. Everything is going fine. Everyone thinks the product will sell well, that it'll be a big money-maker for the company. Then it happens. The fellow from Research and Development casually mentions that they've gotten three letters from people from the area where they've been testing the product. Seems they got a rash after using it. One was hospitalized briefly.

Three letters. Nothing, you say. Absolutely nothing to worry about. We should go right ahead. If we press the button today, we can be out in the market before August!

Silence. The meeting tone has changed. Very, very cool. The importance value of the project has shifted. Where before everything was "go ahead," now each member finds something that suggests a delay. More product testing. Perhaps more evaluation of the advertising. Maybe we should look at the packaging again . . . and do we have enough consumer research . . .?

Why? The skeleton. . . .

If you'd looked back in the history of the company, you'd find that in 1966 they were cited

137

by the FDA for a product that damaged the skin of a number of users. The product had to be withdrawn from the market. There were extended law suits, big money settlements, and the president lost his job!

The letters reported by R&D flashed the red light and the meeting group retrenched. History had sensitized them in this area. And you had not done your homework.

Had you known of this skeleton, you might have been able to suggest an alternate plan that would have allayed the group's fears but would still have let the project go ahead. Now this delay will be a long one. If the product goes at all. The tide has ebbed.

One more example. You rush to a meeting to announce that you've won the Merlin Cosmetic account for your advertising agency—single-handedly. The biggest accomplishment of your young career. After the announcement you sit back to enjoy the praise that's bound to follow.

Stony silence. Just staring eyes. No applause.

Someone asks whether the treasurer has checked the cost to the agency of handling such an account. Another asks about Merlin's share of the cosmetic market. Isn't it going down? Another about the image of Merlin with the trade. All questions, and no one pats you on the back and says, "Great job, Sue."

Sometime back the president of your agency stated that there were two kinds of accounts that he would never, *never* have in the shop because *he* personally didn't think they were the kind of businesses the agency should be involved with. The first was cosmetics. The importance value of your great coup has deflated like a punctured balloon.

It doesn't make any difference if the president is wrong or biased. That's the way he feels, and that's why that hush settled over the meeting when you rushed in with the great news. There's nothing to do about it now. You've lost credibility. *Next* time, probe beforehand for all the skeletons in your company. You'll be intrigued by what you find, and it'll help you avoid the toughest fight you'll ever face—the fight to change an already set policy. Without knowing past history you don't stand a chance.

Search out all the skeletons. They're in every company and they exert *big* power on the

139

positions people take. When you get to know where the bones are buried, you'll have to decide if it's possible to win your way.

The skeletons in the closet can rattle even the best idea.

Remember, No Two People Are Alike

Perhaps the greatest delusion the meeting member can suffer is that all the people present have the same basic position. Since they all started from the same facts, they can only differ in that they want to hear someone else present their point of view. Then they can agree gracefully.

Nothing could be more false. And nothing will mislead you more in the meeting situation. It's a costly mistake to make. You will approach your meeting unprepared for reality. You will lose credibility. You will certainly lose the meeting.

Here is the way I approach a meeting. I automatically assume that each member has gathered his facts from *different* sources. I assume that each person has a *different* point of view, a *different* objective. I assume each person will hold *different* parts of the problem more strongly than others and will probably fight for them to the death. With the exception of the fact that all the people around the table probably have two arms and two legs and one head, I look on them as being separate individuals. This approach has many advantages and you would do well to adopt it.

First, and most important, this view of your colleagues prevents you from looking at the meeting as a Pollyanna land where all share an altruistic view of what is progress and action. (Yours, of course.)

Second, being sensitive to the fact that each meeting member is different makes you try even harder to tailor your ideas to individuals rather than to a homogeneous group.

Third, it keeps the explosion fuse in your head from lighting prematurely. People who believe that unanimity of thought exists in a group tend to blow up quickly when they think they've answered *all* the questions any sensible person could ask. They come to think the listeners are simply being difficult, not wanting to understand. This

142

can lead to big, *big* fights, fights you can't win with anger.

Fourth, recognizing the individuality of thought in a group makes you conscious of the fact that you must persuade the group *one at a time* before you begin to group them. This calls for a flexibility of approach and logic. It's a great feeling to see the individual meeting members come over to your side as a meeting progresses. It's a good measurement of your effectiveness.

So, the next time you go to a meeting, sit back and imagine that the members as they come through the door are coming up the ramp of the Ark. Each one different not in form but in mind and in how they see the problem they're going to discuss shortly. And think that this difference doesn't make your job of convincing them more difficult, it makes it easier; they're individuals with individual thoughts, who can be individually persuaded. Believe me, it's better talking to individuals than talking to a wall of unified resistance.

I urge you to begin the meeting with a simple foundation of fact: Meeting members do not come to the meeting all thinking the way you do even when they have the same basic information. And they rarely come to the meeting table united. They are individuals and individuals are by nature different.

When you look around the table, think about them this way. It will help you form your plan of action. It will help you win the meeting.

The "Eyes" Have It

If you need to be reminded—we live in a visual world. We learn, understand, and are conditioned by the myriad of things we see around us each day. Hearing is an important sense, but compared with the effect of the sense of sight, it's a long way back. It's been estimated that we learn perhaps 90 percent of what we know through our sense of sight. Doesn't it seem paradoxical then that the biggest and undoubtedly most important communication situation we face—the meeting—is almost totally verbal, and therefore appeals to our auditory sense?

There is no doubt that "seeing" reinforces belief. One of our common phrases to someone we doubt is "show me." Or another, when we wish to hammer home a point, is "here, let me show you what I mean." What we really are dealing with in this book is how to make your ideas bear more weight, how to add impact and conviction to what you say. Woodrow Wilson once said:

"Facts do not threaten, they OPERATE."

And *visual* facts operate more strongly than others!

Therefore, one very important way to increase your chance of winning the meeting is to use visuals to hype your good, solid facts, to put those facts in a visual vehicle that will carry them quickly—and directly—into the heads of your listeners.

Here are a few thoughts on the use of visuals in the meeting. If you follow them, I guarantee your meeting success rate will increase substantially.

When should I use visuals? Turn this question around. Is there a reason *not* to use visuals to prove your point? For instance, if the point you're making is *so* simple, visuals may be unnecessary. But is it that simple and dramatic? Frankly, almost all meetings would benefit from use of visuals. Take advantage of this technique

What kind of visual should I use? Again, let the complexity of the subject and the formality of the meeting help determine this. An ordinary newsprint pad on an easel or a blackboard is more than adequate for some presentations. An overhead projector is a very flexible aid that allows you to prepare your visuals on transparencies and project them on a screen or meeting-room wall. For a formal meeting, developed a long time in advance, slides may be more appropriate, or even film. Let judgment of what you need to say and who you're going to say it to help you decide the visual aid to use. Always keep your mind on what you want to say and accomplish. The visual is, after all, only a *support* of your ideas. As Robert Frost once said,

> "You don't go on the tennis court to see if the lines are straight. You go there to play tennis."

Should I sit or stand when making a visual presentation? Always stand. It gives you more authority and will get you more attention and respect. When you stand, you command, and you'll find your ideas are challenged less often.

If I'm using a projector, should the room be

light or dark? Don't work in the dark. In the dark the visual becomes the center of attention and not you. If darkness is needed for film, arrange to have a light on you to keep your position of importance.

Should I develop charts there in front of the meeting audience or prepare the visuals beforehand? If the idea or ideas are simple, it's effective to develop them before the audience. It adds to the attention-grasping quality. People love to see things happen before their eyes. If it's complicated, of course, you must prepare beforehand. If you do this, think of covering parts of your charts with strips of paper and revealing information as the idea progresses. It's a good dramatic ploy.

How "finished" should my visuals be? Again, you must use your judgment according to the subject and the audience. This much we can say for sure: Listeners don't expect presenters to be artists. It's the content that counts. There may even be an extra plus for the "rougher" visual. Listeners feel it's closer to the thinking of the speaker and that the importance has been put on the thoughts, not the execution. Warning, however: Be neat and orderly.

148

How to Win the Meeting

How much should I put on a chart? Only *one* idea. Putting up an amalgam of confusing numbers or visualizations defeats the very purpose of using visuals to make listeners "see" your points more easily.

Is there any single trick that will help in using visuals? Yes! Always simplify your ideas. By that I mean take your numbers, ideas, points and put them in the most easily understood visual form, such as this simple bar graph from *The New York Times*, for instance. Ths visual is much more immediate than the numbers alone.

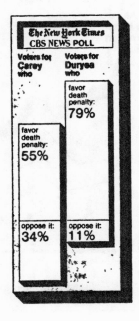

Or this pictograph of Iran's oil output. Note how immediate the difference in oil flow becomes.

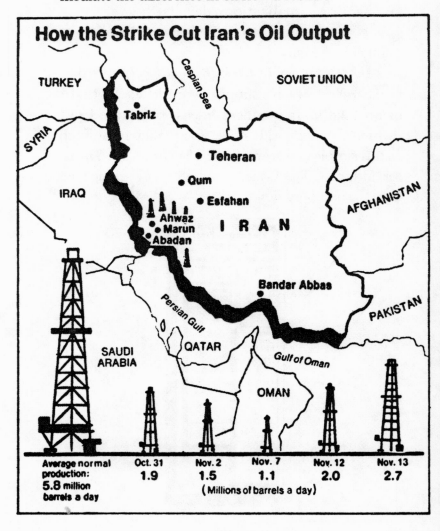

How the Strike Cut Iran's Oil Output

TURKEY

Caspian Sea

SOVIET UNION

• Tabriz

SYRIA

• Teheran

IRAQ

• Qum

• Esfahan

AFGHANISTAN

Ahwaz
• Marun
• Abadan

I R A N

Bandar Abbas

PAKISTAN

Persian Gulf

SAUDI
ARABIA

QATAR

Gulf of Oman

OMAN

| Average normal production: 5.8 million barrels a day | Oct. 31 1.9 | Nov. 2 1.5 | Nov. 7 1.1 | Nov. 12 2.0 | Nov. 13 2.7 |

(Millions of barrels a day)

How to Win the Meeting

Or this dramatic comparison by Steinway & Sons showing the choice of their pianos by soloists.

AGAIN.

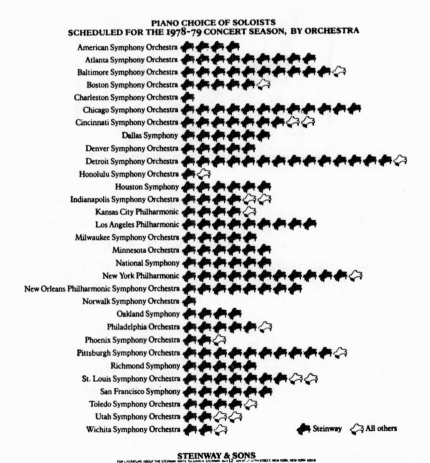

PIANO CHOICE OF SOLOISTS
SCHEDULED FOR THE 1978-79 CONCERT SEASON, BY ORCHESTRA

STEINWAY & SONS
FOR LITERATURE ABOUT THE STEINWAY WRITE TO JOHN H. STEINWAY, BOX 12, STEINWAY HALL, 109 WEST 57TH STREET, NEW YORK, NEW YORK 10019

151

And finally, this visualization of the dramatic swing of the prime rate in *Business Week*.

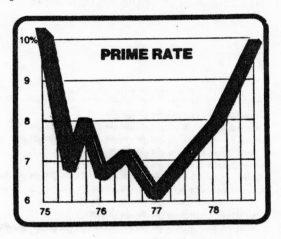

Go to your local art supply store. Look over all the materials (pads, crayons, magic markers, color tapes, etc.) available for your use on visuals in the meeting. Get to know your supplier. He'll be helpful in advising you. It will be a trip well taken.

Take advantage of the power *seeing* can give you in your speaking. Just because visuals may not be used in most of the meetings you attend isn't a reason for you *not* to use them. It's a reason *for* you to use them.

Show 'Em How It Works

Show and Tell is the part of school more young kids come home and tell their parents about than any other. The reason is simple: Children are eye oriented. They like to be shown things, to have objects held up and talked about. And we're no different from the kids. In any situation when someone holds up something, all eyes immediately rivet on it. Attention is instantly focused. What everybody tries to do with words just doesn't work as well as the showing of the object itself. In short, everyone loves a "show."

Let's start by talking technique. How to show an object in a meeting to make your point clearer, more immediate, more vital. It's relatively simple . . . but there *is* a right and wrong way of doing it.

When most people attempt to show an object,

they approach it as if they think it pornographic, as if they were embarrassed by what the audience is eager to see. The probable reason? So few people demonstrate objects in the meeting to prove their points that meeting members think they're doing something odd . . . using a technique that's not quite kosher.

Nonsense!

There are critical times in the meeting when the object itself is by far the quickest clincher of an argument. Nothing else will do the job as well. But, as I said earlier, you must know how to use this technique. Here are a few suggestions.

When you've decided to show an object in a meeting, bring it to the meeting openly. Don't attempt to hide it in your pocket. Don't try to cover it up. Don't put it under your chair. Just place it on the table in front of you. People will notice it, but it will just make them pay more attention to you, wondering when you'll show it to them.

Don't play with the object before you're ready to describe it. Reaching for it, fondling it, putting it down, and reaching for it again will do nothing but drive your watchers crazy. And make them hate you for the uncertainty.

When you do demonstrate the object, hold it in front of you naturally—chest high, being careful that all at the table have a good view. If you notice someone craning to see, make a special effort to bring it into his vision. You'll make a friend and hopefully a supporter.

Move the object slowly, as if you too were examining it. Be interested in the object, treat it with respect. So many speakers ask their listeners to look at something, and then throw the object aside as if it was something to be disdained. Bad.

Point to the part of the object you wish to show. Remember, you're leading the viewer's sight through the object, they *must* follow you. Turn it over. Point out parts or areas or functions. Think of yourself as a guide at the United Nations, pointing out things of interest to people who've never been there before.

When you're finished with the object, put it down and don't touch it again—unless you find it

155

necessary to demonstrate it again. Then do it again with the same care and personal interest as before.

Never, never pass the object around the room. Don't let the listeners examine it *as* you describe it. From the moment you do, you'll have no listeners. They won't hear a word you say. All eyes will be on the object, examining it or waiting to examine it. You'll have lost your audience completely.

Practice at home. If you're going to show how something works, don't go through a big buildup, gather all attention, and then discover that the object doesn't work. You'll have lost the meeting, to say nothing of your credibility.

Next time you want to make a point that will be helped by showing an object, jump at the chance. You'll be amazed at the attention you'll get. People just naturally love to see physical things, things they can examine and be told about. Harness this little-used device. It'll give you a big leg up in winning the meeting.

Find a Rallying Cry

"... man does not live in a world of hard facts, or according to his immediate needs or desires. He lives rather in the midst of his imaginary emotions, in hopes and fears, in illusions and disillusions, in his fantasies and dreams."
—ERNST CASSIRER

The great movements of history, famous and infamous, have been started by individuals who put together a simple combination of words that could not be resisted. In 1095, in response to a speech by Pope Urban II regarding the wisdom of beginning the First Crusade, the assembly shouted:

"Deus vult" (God wills it!)

Armed with this emotional plea, Peter the hermit raised a giant army and brought them to battle

and death on the road to Jerusalem. What a cry¹
And what persuasion!

Winston Churchill, with England beaten almost
to its knees, offered the people

"... blood, toil, tears and sweat!"

To this rallying cry, the English dug in, fought,
and won the war.

In the dark years of the Depression, Roosevelt,
knowing the land was confused and fearful, told
the people,

"The only thing we have to fear is fear itself."

And the great American Depression was on its
way to being overcome.

A rallying cry. Something that touches listeners,
something they can remember, a combination of
words that crystallizes the subject. Words people
can empathize with and feel a part of, words that
make them part of the group and not alone, convince them that they *can* win, and will.

You should consider this technique as a way to
give your ideas greater horsepower, the power of
uniqueness and memorability, extra power
because it is so seldom used in the meeting
situation.

In politics, where the emotional appeal sways masses, you hear the rallying cry used constantly. As in President Johnson's "Great Society," Roosevelt's "New Deal," New York's "Big Apple." In advertising, it's with us every day: "The Pepsi Generation," "The Friendly Skies of United," "Breakfast of Champions," and many, many more.

And why is the rallying cry used so often? Because it works.

If you want to harness a seldom-used technique to win the meeting and see your ideas put into action, try the rallying cry in your next meeting. But its use takes preparation. You must develop the "cry" you want to use before the meeting because the statement must be carefully tuned to the meeting, the listeners, and, of course, the subject. For instance:

The rallying cry must fit the tone and tenor and importance of the meeting subject. A "march-to-victory" statement is too overblown for a drive to gain additional distribution for a laundry detergent. But giving it the rallying cry of the "wash-day blitz" lumps it together in vivid language that everyone can remember, accept, and respond to.

A rallying cry must be within the common

knowledge of all you expect to use it. They must understand it easily. It's got to be an instant signal. Suppose you are trying to get townspeople to band together to clean up the town's parks. You wouldn't call it "Augean Task Force" (after the stable in mythology cleaned out by Hercules). No one would understand. But you might call it "Operation Clean Sweep!"

The rallying cry should incorporate an emotional idea as well as a descriptive one. For instance, if you've been trying to convince the town fathers that the town needs to plan and clean up for the coming town festival, you might use the rallying cry of "Spruce-up Month." But it could have more impact if you build in an emotional word for extra power, such as "Town *Pride* Month."

The rallying cry is a common tool of many groups in our society who want to win acceptance of their views. The use of a rallying cry can help you be remembered in the meeting. And if you're remembered, you have a better chance of gathering in the meeting members' votes.

160

One Final Note

I have never equivocated on the object of this book. It was written to help you win the meeting, to give you techniques that will help you see your positions prevail, your ideas put into effect.

And there are a lot of meetings to win, lots of good ideas that need to be accepted if our relatively good life is to prevail. More and more people are going to have to find ways to move their good ideas through groups of people if we are not to come to a standstill. The anti-nuclear-power proponents need to persuade more people that they're right. So do those who say we need all kinds of power to maintain a healthy, growing country. Both sides must learn to get more people

161

involved . . . and convinced. Both have got to learn to present convincing support and win their points . . . to win this big meeting of minds.

Bad ideas? I don't worry about them. If everyone learns to push his ideas with more force and logic, the bad ideas will fall by themselves. Hitler could never have come to power if those opposing him were forcefully selling their ideas to the German public. In 1859, Charles Darwin published a book that shook the world to its foundations. *Origin of Species* set forth the then astonishing idea that the human being evolved from a far more primitive state. It caused quite a stir! But it's the premise of this book that's important. The creatures that survive are those that best fit their environment, best do the job the environment demands. There's a lesson here.

We have lots of problems to solve. The Mideast conflict, unemployment, Mary Williams and her marketing group, the new product your subsidiary wants to introduce, Bill Jones and the school board. There's no shortage of problems that need solutions to make our life better and more rewarding.

How to Win the Meeting

Remember, the best-suited creatures survive to change the present and the future.

Win the meeting!